I WILL NOT BE IGNORED

Ed Friedman

Cover: Design by Dwayne Booth

Book layout by HumorOutcasts Press.

Published 2024 by HumorOutcasts Press

Printed in the United States of America

ISBN: 979-8-9894863-3-5

Acknowledgements

I am grateful to editors Roz Warren and Kathryn Taylor who steered me in the right direction, especially since I rarely know where I'm going. Many thanks to Donna Cavanagh at Humor Outkast for helping with final decisions and Dwayne Booth for his artwork and patience. I've learned so much from Janine Annett, Dan Zevin and all the folks at the Sarah Lawrence Writing Institute. A special thank you to Tessa Smith McGovern whose guidance and encouragement led to the creation of this book. Thanks to the Writers on the Sound for their feedback and fellowship; and Arty Conliffe, who encourages me to think more deeply in and outside the box.

And of course, Allison Jaffe, whose very presence in my life means that I won't be a tortured writer, but instead, a relatively happy one.

Or, as happy as I'm ever going to be.

Introduction

You've made it this far.

I'm not assuming you've purchased this book as yet. (If you have, thank you) It could be that you're standing in the aisle of a bookstore or browsing Amazon, and you were drawn to the title, the description, or the artwork, and decided to read the introduction to see if you're interested. That's not particularly funny, but then again, it's hard to know what makes people laugh, chuckle, or smile.

In 1978 I was sitting in a movie theatre on East 68th Street in Manhattan watching *La Cage aux Folles*. (This was long before it became a Broadway musical, and before it was transformed into the movie, *The Birdcage.*) In the film, the character of Albin, in an effort to appear more stereotypically masculine, puts on a conventional grey suit.

However, he crosses his legs to reveal bright pink socks. The audience roared. I found the scene touching and could not understand why people were laughing.

That should be, I suppose, a cautionary tale when it comes to writing a humor book. However, not having a formula for what most people find funny, my solution is to write stuff that I find funny and hope that most of it lands with people who read it.

This book is divided up as follows: a bunch of stories that I've invented for no good reason other than they made me laugh to read them; episodes from my life that strike me as amusing; and some opinions and observations that strike me as funny. Also, a bunch of other people read these and told me they were funny. Either that or they didn't want to hurt my feelings.

In the comic plays I've written, it's easy to sit in the audience and listen for laughs or the dreaded silence. Since I can't stand behind you when you're reading this book (luckily for you *and* me), I'm just going to imagine that, while it is unlikely everyone will laugh at everything, everybody (including you) will laugh at something.

If you're still undecided about whether or not to buy the book, take the leap. If you like it, please tell your friends. But tell them you've misplaced your copy, so they'll have to buy their own.

Table of Contents

Section One: THINGS THAT HAPPENED

Bad Food

Keep It Away from Me

For much of my life beets were a non-issue. They were not a featured vegetable. (It's a vegetable, right? Just checking.) I actually never saw beets as I was growing up. The only exception was when they made an appearance in something called borscht. Borscht is a traditional Russian beet soup that includes other vegetables, potatoes, onions, chicken broth, and some kind of meat. But it's mostly beets. It can be served either hot or cold. The soup's color is a deep red. The smell is something that would drive me from any room I'm in.

I had one dramatic encounter with borscht. It was sixty years ago but it is burned into my mind.

My parents had a semi-attached home in the Bronx with what we called a "finished basement." This below ground floor of the house contained a half bath, a small kitchen, a storage room, a workshop, and a larger room with a (never used) bar. The room opened up to a good-sized yard.My parents occasionally entertained in the basement and yard, which meant all the food cooked and stored upstairs had to be brought down to the basement.

On one such occasion, my sister and brothers, and I, as usual, were the unpaid staff. We were tasked with fetching any party supplies, drinks, and food. At one point I was asked to transport a huge Tupperware vat of borscht that barely fit in the upstairs refrigerator to the basement. With the cover on the Tupperware, I was spared the aroma I detested so much, but with only three steps to go before I could hand off the offending substance, I tripped, and the entire contents of the Tupperware was everywhere including all over me. I could barely hear my stepmother screaming at me over the debilitating attack on my olfactory senses. At that point I was convinced that nothing less than a "Silkwood Scrub" would remove the offending odor. Suffice it to say, since then I would no doubt give up the launch codes to nuclear missiles were I forced to eat a beet.

I've gone on to successfully avoid beets my entire adult life. I've been to friends' homes for dinner, out to restaurants, attended weddings and all manner of parties and I never saw a beet on anyone's plate. Then about ten years ago I noticed something different. Beet salad started to show up on restaurant menus. Other salads now included beets. And people were eating them. At one point I found myself at a table with people I considered my friends, talking about how much they loved beets.

Madness.

Seltzer

I don't get seltzer. Whether it's called club soda, sparkling water, or is made by a French-sounding company and comes in bright green bottles, it's just water that makes you burp. And it has no flavor. And if you order it in a restaurant you have to pay for it, which you don't have to do with just water, WHICH THE RESTAURANT AUTOMATICALLY GIVES TO YOU.

My wife loves club soda (and I married her anyway). We used to have cases of it in the apartment until she found something called SodaStream. This is a machine that makes seltzer by use of CO_2 cannisters inserted into a plastic structure. The machine comes with bottles which, after being filled with water (yes, free), are inserted into the machine. After pressing down on the button on the machine six or seven times, you have a bottle of seltzer. The cannisters lose their ability to aerate after a few months and you have to buy new ones, which are getting harder to find. So, it still costs money, but I'm not tripping over cases of bubbly water.

Too Bad to Eat

"Oh God, this is horrible," is what I thought as I reluctantly swallowed a bite of food from what was purported to be the best Chinese restaurant in Pontiac, Michigan. I'm a born and bred New Yorker and had been eating Chinese food all my life. In my experience, Chinese food in restaurants from lower Manhattan to the North Bronx varied between "great" and "okay."

This food would have to improve by a power of ten to reach okay. "Why are you still chewing?" you may ask. Well, first of all, I was very hungry. The last leg of a car trip from Ohio was made without a food stop, so I would probably have eaten the first edition of *Wuthering Heights* if it were seasoned properly. Secondly, the pride of our Michigan hosts in introducing us to, in their estimation, the height of culinary accomplishment was inestimable. We were to be their guests for the next ten days, much of it spent recalling childhood memories. I certainly didn't want to begin our stay by expressing judgment and dissatisfaction.

So I chewed and swallowed, hoping against hope that one of our hosts wouldn't ask, "So how do you like it?"

Lest you think I'm some kind of food snob, my favorite place to eat is a diner where food is simple and unambitious (not unlike myself).

If I'm honest, what I can be snobby about is pizza. Living in the pizza capital of the world (I'm sorry, Chicago, what you have is some kind of pie that you can't put ice cream on), I'm privy to the best of the ultimate comfort food. I've never had a bad slice of pizza.

Then again, I've never had pizza in Pontiac, Michigan.

Human Maintenance

It was as if all my body parts got together to give me a terrible surprise. Unlike major league baseball owners, body parts can't be taken to court for collusion. Turning fifty was much more dramatic than I ever expected. Up to that point, I was oblivious to the idea of getting older. There were a few preliminary signs but somehow, they didn't faze me: the need for reading glasses at forty-five didn't bother me since practically everyone I knew had been wearing glasses or contacts for some time; even my receding hairline was something I could ignore. It wasn't until I found myself in a friend's bathroom (with more mirrors than I find necessary), that I saw what I can only describe as a large hole in the back of my head. My head was still there (I know because I instinctively went to touch it) but there was this vacant spot where hair used to be. I kept touching the empty area as if my eyes were deceiving me.

But there was no avoiding the truth—I was well on my way to being bald. You may ask, how could you not have known? The truth is I stopped looking at the back of my head as a teenager, after which I kept my hair either too long or too short to make a difference what the back looked like. Before that, I checked out the back of my head in hopes of forming a "d.a." (If you're too young to know what that is, google the movies "Cry-Baby" or "Hairspray.") So, if I avoided the homes of my design-challenged friends I wouldn't have to look at the back of my head and could successfully evade the entire issue.

Ironically, or by nature's vendetta, as I lost hair where I hoped to retain it, I found myself sprouting hair like a ChiaPet in places I had absolutely no interest in doing so. Seemingly overnight my ears, nose, and eyebrows started to look like the Brazilian rain forest. One might say "the Lord giveth and the Lord taketh away." I say how about the Lord just leaveth everything where the hell it is. I see no biological imperative for this phenomenon, and it benefits no one— except the folks that sell hair replacement methods and electronic nose hair clippers, a device which, I might add, was given to me by my loving partner. Now if we're getting ready to go out, I'm likely to hear, "Honey, you might want to check your ears and your nose." My reply to the first time this question was asked— "no problem, they're still there"— was met with the tilted head, and a silent "be good and take your medicine" look.

I can avoid facing the hairy thing I'm about to be if I just don't put my glasses on. Reading glasses were a small but annoying concession to my age. What has occurred since is the realization that this is a progressive condition and the three-for-ten-dollars Walgreens glasses have given way to a prescription for a pair that allows me to complete the Times crossword (OK, work on the Times crossword) and read the obituaries in the vain hope that I've outlived someone I actually know. These glasses also allow me to read advertisements for medications used to treat conditions I never heard of with side effects that are worse than the disease. The first cholesterol medication I was given had terrific results. However, subsequent blood tests revealed that if I stayed on this regimen my liver would explode. Out with that medication and in with a weight loss program that subsequently had the effect of reducing my cholesterol. So that's taken care of, right?

Not so fast. Some years later, chest pains that wouldn't go away sent me to an emergency room. Now before I go any further, I should inject some background. My family history is a red flag for every doctor I see. My mother died at thirty-one with stomach cancer and my father died at fifty-three from a heart attack that followed two strokes. Naturally, everybody wants to test me for everything. So it was no surprise when the emergency room doctor said, "With your medical history… (Every doctor who talks to me begins with those four words) … we should admit you for some testing." So now I'm lying in the emergency room, wired up like Clockwork Orange for about six hours, then unplugged, wheeled to another room, and replugged. After being woken at regular intervals (to see if I was alive?), I was sent for an echocardiogram, during which the person administering the test had an argument with one of the doctors. It was of no small concern to me that someone administering a test that would have life-altering consequences would be distracted and pissed off. Therefore, given the choice of taking a stress test then or the following week, I took the latter option.

The point of a stress test seems to be the answer to the question "How long can you jog on a treadmill at increasing speeds, with wires attached to you, before you scream or drop dead?" I'm sure it was a bitter disappointment to the doctors that I didn't die and was too busy gasping for air to scream. The result of all the testing is that I've been prescribed high blood pressure medication, cholesterol medication, and, in case of chest pains, nitroglycerin. The comment "You probably won't need this, it's just in case" didn't inspire confidence. Instead, I imagined myself in a 1940s noir thriller where the wife can save her rich older husband or let him die by not giving him the nitro. Fortunately, my economic status exempts me from being a player in this scenario. The conclusion was that I should do something about my stress. Even though I was not suicidal or psychotic, I still qualified for a low-level anti-depressant, which, while not preventing the nighttime bathroom trips, allows me to fall back to sleep instead of spending the rest of the night worrying about why I can't fall back to sleep.

My current medications are successfully keeping my heart from exploding and will continue to work, according to my cardiologist. Never in my life did I think I would utter the words "my cardiologist."

I always thought phrases like that only came from people on buses on the way home from Atlantic City. But in fact, I do have a cardiologist, and a nephrologist, a urologist (more on that later), an ophthalmologist a gastroenterologist, a psychiatrist, an internist, and four dentists of varying specialties. I wound up assembling this team when, after years of neglect, my teeth and gums decided to get even. When I finally broke down and found a dentist, (based on a recommendation from someone to whom I am so longer speaking) his diagnosis, while upsetting, was made even more so from the sticker shock of what it would cost me to repair my gums and keep my remaining teeth from falling out. I was able to find another dentist who, while confirming the diagnosis, came with a smaller price tag. Not cheap, but I would still be able to have a roof over my head, if not much else. As they used to say about Hollywood blockbusters, my path to dental health was "years in the making." I endured gum surgeries, root canals, and implants. Along with these came admonishments about flossing. Just when I thought I was done with my voluntary torture—I wasn't. But in the midst of this, I was fortunately distracted by a new set of medical miseries.

Apparently, another byproduct of turning fifty for some men (and by some men I mean me) is the dreaded enlarged prostate. While not life-threatening, the effect of an enlarged prostate is that the bladder doesn't empty, hence a tremendous increase in the number of trips to the bathroom. Eventually, the two or three interruptions of sleep each night became, if not tolerable, certainly expected. Where this really puts a crimp in your life is the knowledge that humiliation and wet pants are just a bad traffic jam away. Since I had once again ignored a problem in its early stages, the anxiety and fear just exacerbated the problem. (Did I mention that stress just increases the urgency?) My first trip to the urologist was educational: "no coffee, no caffeine, no chocolate." (Kill me now.) Nevertheless, I was determined to see if a simple diet change would change my life. No such luck. The next step was medication. This was easy, I thought. "Let me tell you about the side effects," Dr. F said. "You may experience a dry mouth, and...well...let's just say you won't be able to star in any pornographic movies." This was the doctor's delicate way of telling me that the medication would preclude the production of sperm at ejaculation. Since I had long retired from the porn business this wasn't an issue. (Yes, that's a joke.) While the doctor was finished letting me down easy with respect to my future in the cinema, he also expressed the need to make sure I didn't have bladder cancer. To do that, I would have to have a cystoscopy. This consists of inserting a tube into the penis and, since I was almost blacked out from the pain, I have no idea what the doctor was doing during this procedure. My only recollection is of him trying to give me instructions (mainly to keep me from hyperventilating and moving), during which he referred to me as "Sir." Now I'm all for civility and doctors respecting patients, but I was struck by the fact that here I was, half-naked and lying there with a tube up my penis, and we weren't even on a first-name basis. I was sure there wouldn't be a second date. When the agony finally ended, it didn't. I had to survive two days of pain whenever I urinated, which was…well, you get the idea. I continued the medication for some time, during which the sum of benefits I received were the side effects.

As if all this wasn't enough, my regular doctor uttered the familiar intro, "given your family history," and added, "you should have a colonoscopy." Being sufficiently scared and filling a void with no one digging around my mouth or my crotch, I faced up to the inevitable. The good news about this procedure is that the patient is given an anesthetic, which for all intents and purposes renders one unconscious. Generally, there are no after-effects except a little grogginess that goes away when the anesthetic wears off. The bad news (you just knew there was going to be bad news, didn't you?) is that in order for the doctors to ogle your insides, your insides have to be clear. That means you must spend the better part of the twenty-four hours before the procedure "emptying" everything inside you. To achieve this, you're given a hideous tasting concoction to drink at six-hour intervals, along with instructions to eat nothing except Jell-O (not the red kind) and drink only clear liquids. You will spend the next eighteen hours as a prisoner to your bathroom passing everything, including, it seems, all your internal organs. If the preparation sounds worse than the test, you have a complete understanding of the colonoscopy.

All these measures make trivial the conditions with which I've been living for a long time. One is a bad lower back for which I see a chiropractor who mercifully sticks nothing into me and whose treatments are not at all invasive. Apparently, if I keep my weight down and move around occasionally, I should be all right. But every once and a while I feel a twinge back there; or some pain from where I had the hernia surgery (at age fifty-one); or foot cramps, constipation, tooth pain, gas, allergic reaction; or just some ache that comes out of nowhere, lasts for thirty seconds, then disappears. I remember telling the psychiatrist, "The biggest difference between being thirty and sixty is that when you're thirty you take your body for granted. You just don't question how it works or that someday it won't. Now, every day it feels like I'm aware of a new body part and how it functions or doesn't." He replied, "If you're over fifty and you wake up and nothing hurts, you've died in your sleep."

For some reason I find this terribly comforting.

In Memoriam

It's been over forty years, and I still can't believe she's gone. What great times we had. Staying up all night talking. Laughing uncontrollably. I certainly never had that kind of fun again. Sure, some of the "morning afters" were rough, but it was so worth it.

Of course, I'm talking about cocaine.

Weekends were a blur back then. (We only indulged on the weekends.) From Friday through Sunday we were surrounded by friends with whom we spent hours talking, going to parties, dancing and arriving at what we felt were lofty intellectual pronouncements. Gun to my head, I couldn't tell you even one.

Ah, those were the days. I'm sure I now sound like the guys who frequented what we used to call the "old man bars." They'd lecture us on gender roles (not that they used that term), and how the neighborhood had changed. Now I'm the old guy and I hang out at Dunkin Donuts.

But when I can't manage to keep my eyes open past 9:30, I find myself thinking, ''Wouldn't it be nice to have a few lines right now?'' Then I think:

How much does cocaine cost these days?

Back in the eighties it was expensive, and we pooled our money to get some. Now, it's probably the cost of a mortgage payment.

Where would I even get it?

I have no idea what happened to my connection. He could be dead for all I know (possible); in jail (very possible); or Entertainment Director for Princess Cruises (extremely likely, he was very charming).

Wouldn't it be great to be surrounded by all those people again?

Everybody is your friend when you're holding. (Well, yeah, I know that now. I wonder what did happen to all those people)?

What could we have possibly been talking about for so long?

I love my friends dearly, but our intellectual curiosity did not extend past the larger message of *Return of the Jedi*. It is extremely unlikely that we would have arrived at any profound philosophical insights.

What would happen if I actually got my hands on some?

Would I be even more manic with the remote? My wife already thinks I have an attention deficit disorder.

Would my wife do some with me? Yeah…no. She's a bit of a control freak (Also, see above).

Would it be dangerous at my age? Given that I'm under the care of a cardiologist, I'm pretty sure he would tell me that my heart would explode.

Who would I share it with? Well, the wife is out. Every one of my other friends is on blood pressure meds, beta blockers, or blood thinners, so I'm going to say, no one.

What would I do if I had some coke right now?

I suppose I could binge watch *The Wire* and *Breaking Bad*, which everyone raves about, but I never got to see.

Or I could crank out a bunch of short missives, which, in my cocaine-fueled brain, I would find hysterically funny, but which, in fact, are mildly amusing.

Instant Theatre-Just Add Coffee

I looked at the ad three times. Each time I did, I put the newspaper down, but something kept drawing me back to it:

Westchester theatre seeks actors, directors, and playwrights for 24-hour Marathon.

I always wanted to write a play. While I'd seen these marathons promoted in Off-Off-Broadway theatres, I always told myself this wasn't for me. And it was too much of a hassle to get downtown. Now, this would be in Westchester, where I live.

What was I afraid of? Only that:

a) I would never be able to write a play, overnight.

b) I would have my worst fear, that I have no talent, confirmed.

c) I would suffer abject humiliation, and as a result...

d) ...I would never be able to leave my house in the light of day again

And yet I still want to move forward and try and write a play, so I leaped into action.

Not really. I procrastinated.

When my wife told me that the shelf paper in the kitchen cabinets did not need to be changed, again I was out of excuses. I pulled up the theatre's online application form, answered a few brief questions, and I was done. Although I don't see how answering "Who is your favorite character from Harry Potter?" tells anybody anything. Not having read the books or seen any of the movies, I googled Harry Potter. I picked Prof. Severus Snape, only because he was played by Alan Rickman. I still didn't know who the character was and prayed to God that no one would ask me about it. Still, there was a very good chance that I wouldn't be accepted which meant I wouldn't have to face my fear of failure.

But, alas, three days later, while girding myself for rejection, I received an e-mail instructing me to show up at the theatre on the following Friday at 7:00. While part of me was excited, most of me felt the way I did when I received the notice from my draft board telling me to report for my army physical. At least, I told myself, I wouldn't be nearly naked this time-it would just feel that way.

The way the Marathon works is that people apply as either a playwright, actor, or director. They meet at the theatre at 7 pm on a Friday evening. No one knows each other. The organizer randomly puts people in small groups consisting of a playwright, a director, and actors. After an hour-long "getting to know you" period, the playwright goes off and writes. They have until 7:00 the next morning to complete a 10-minute play. The director and actors show up the next morning and are given the scripts to work on until showtime-7 P.M. that night. If I can't produce anything, the people on my team will be screwed, and my fear of failure will be realized.

No pressure.

I've always been intrigued by these projects. They appeal to my sense of needing a deadline in order to write anything, my lack of commitment to any long-term project, and my abject boredom with anything I've ever created seconds after its completion.

That Friday, I expected a large turnout of experienced theatre-makers and was prepared to be intimidated, which I hoped would fuel my resolve, and jump-start my creativity. Instead, I walked into the cavernous theatre to find fourteen other people representing various levels of experience, age, and ethnicity.

The theatre's Education Coordinator was a young energetic woman named Tracey. Tracey had the personality of a governor's press secretary who believed in all of her boss' bullshit as she waxed rhapsodic about her theatre. She engaged us all in exercises to help us get to know each other, so we could all get an idea about everyone's personality, and how people expressed themselves.

During the exercises I found myself making mental notes like, "She would be interesting," "I like his accent," and, "If you stick me with her, I'll kill myself." But I did get an idea of the talent in the group.

When the pairings were announced, I was partnered with a director, Eloise, who had never directed before but is a playwright — so there was a real possibility that my play would be re-written and badly directed. The actors were two young women from Brooklyn, Lisa, and Paula, in their early 30s. The four of us repaired to a quiet spot to talk. As for the two actors, I soon learned that English was not their first language (French and Portuguese). They'd been in the states for less than two years, but their English was just fine and the women seemed to have a rapport with one another.

We all shared a bit about our experiences in the theatre and how we work, and then we all left the theatre; the actors and director to sleep, and me to write.

By the time I got home and had a quick dinner, it was 10 pm. I had nine hours to write the play and send it on to the director.

There was a time in my life when being up all night was no big deal. (There was also a time in my life that I did cocaine every weekend but that wasn't happening tonight. Also, I believe my dealer is now the social director for a cruise line, so I wouldn't know where to score). But now, it's a big deal. I didn't dare fall asleep as there was no guarantee I'd get up in time to write the play. So fueled with caffeine, I proceeded.

11:00 Panic had already set in, and I made an aborted attempt to retrofit a play I tried to write years ago that has been languishing in a folder.

12:00 I realized why it was still in the folder-it was terrible.

1:00 AM Rejected the idea of a zombie psychotherapist and vampire patient.

2:00 AM I actually get a good idea for a ten-minute play. Thinking about the rapport between Lisa and Paula I stumbled onto a premise: A woman asks a close friend to seduce her husband. (Trust me it's funny, and it has a twist).

4:00 AM I pushed "Send." Truth be told, I wasn't sure the play was ready, but my fatigue had rendered any further revision pointless. As Lorne Michaels once said about Saturday Night Live, "The show doesn't go on because it's ready; it goes on because it's 11:30."

The next day I made it to the theatre an hour before the show. Eloise rushed up to me to ask if she could change a particular word. I don't remember which word — but the meaning was the same and, for some reason, it was easier for the actor to say, so I agreed. Truth be told, at that point I would have agreed to a request that they perform the play speaking Aramaic.

Eloise also explained that there were some cultural references she had to translate for the actors. I didn't stop to ask whether it's because the references were quintessentially American, or because they were born out of pop culture from thirty years ago. One thing I learned from this was when writing for younger actors don't assume they'll know anything about *Hill Street Blues*. Did I really need a reminder of how much older I was than any of these folks? I guess I did.

The plays went on at 7 pm as promised and as with most projects like this, to varying degrees of success. I felt sorry for some of the "actors" (intentional quotes) who, from their expressions, looked as if they had just landed on the stage from Neptune; or the ones who, even with scripts in their hands were incapable of saying their lines. The actors in my play (because let's face it, that's what I was really interested in) did a really good job, as did the director.

Much to my surprise, as I watched, I realized I might have a viable, ten-minute play.

Would I do this again? Maybe. Or maybe I should sit down and without any outside deadline to move me, try to write another play.

But first I think the bathtub needs grouting.

Lost and Found

At some point, you may find yourself driving in the New York metropolitan area and need driving directions. If you spot me, looking like I know where I'm going, I implore you, don't ask me for help. That is, unless you want to drive around aimlessly for the next two hours, cursing me, and re-filling your gas tank. I seem to be constitutionally unable to comprehend driving directions. So, asking me to help you get to where you're going would just be a fool's errand.

I learned to drive late, which is why I'm so bad at directions. Well, that's my story and I'm sticking to it. In any event, I have no other explanation as to why, if I stop at a gas station to ask for directions and the long-suffering service station attendant in the blue jumpsuit with the name "Bob" patched to his pocket (It's always "Bob") says, "Turn right out of here, go two blocks to Pine, make a right for about a quarter-mile, make a left by the school for a few blocks and you'll see an abandoned lot that looks like the entrance to the highway. That's not it. Go another two blocks, make a right and that's where you get on," what

I hear is "lalalalalalalalalala." I simply can't picture what he's talking about, and I certainly can't retain the information.

I should have seen this coming.

When I was seventeen my parents encouraged me to take an aptitude test as they were desperately searching for a direction for me to take post-high school. Their own career suggestions up to that point consisted of undertaker, court reporter, or joining the Coast Guard, none of which had any appeal to me.

While the test was useless in terms of any career guidance, I remember one of its findings quite well. It named several traits and how I ranked percentagewise with people of my age range and education. Let me summarize: Reading Comprehension: Very Good; Verbal Ability, Very Good; Writing Ability, Very Good; Spatial Visualization, Very Very Bad. I was off the charts in the last category and not in a good way.

So maybe I can blame the fact that I can't picture how to get anywhere on an inherited trait. Although I'm sure I didn't get it from my father, as he drove a cab in New York for years while we were growing up in the Bronx.

None of this was that big a deal until my 30s. Before that, I routinely traveled by subway, which thoughtfully provided maps to tell me where to get on and off. Once I exited the public conveyance, I made sure that whoever I was meeting gave me explicit directions, which I held on to like the last canteen of water in the desert. Without those directions, I was literally the wandering Jew.

But then I learned to drive.

Being able to drive opened many possibilities for me, but also a new set of problems. This was before the age of GPS, so I relied on maps. I would plan my route as best I could, writing down the directions in large letters on a legal pad that I placed on the seat next to me. As I had no confidence in either my driving or my mapping, frequently looking down at the directions was probably not the smartest move. None of this improved my competence or confidence behind the wheel.

After a while, I got marginally better about getting around locally.

Then I met Allison, a smart, attractive woman who was everything I looked for…except for the fact that she was living in Fords, New Jersey. Before I could say, "Where the hell is that?" I looked it up on a map I got from Bob at the local gas station. I could easily find Fords and see that it was about ¾ of an inch from the George Washington Bridge. That didn't seem so bad. (My negative grade in Spatial Visualization rears its ugly head.)

Sensitive to my lack of driving experience, and that for me going to New Jersey may as well have been going to North Dakota, Allison gave me explicit directions, which I dutifully wrote down in big letters on a legal pad and put on the seat next to me.

Even I could see that going the ¾ of an inch would take the better part of an hour. I began to wonder whether I should consider Allison "geographically unavailable." But I really liked her. This would be my moment of truth. Would I let my inability to drive without getting hopelessly lost stand in the way of my happiness?

My first trip to Fords went as follows: As I made my way down Henry Hudson Parkway, all was well. By this time, I had a cell phone, which was next to me on the seat with Allison's directions written in big letters on the legal pad. I was well into New Jersey when I glanced down and saw that the upcoming directions included a "jug handle." I was already on Route 1, which mercifully had traffic lights, so I called Allison. As soon as she picked up, I asked, "What the hell is a jug handle?" As it turns out, a jug handle is an exit from a service road that loops around and crosses six lanes of the highway and ultimately results in your going in the opposite direction from the one in which you were driving.

This, to me, was completely counterintuitive, but Allison patiently tried to explain the concept to me as I drove, which was like explaining alternate side of the street parking to a cranberry. She was able to talk me through the rest of the trip. When I finally pulled into the parking lot of her apartment complex, I felt like I had completed a solo moon landing and deserved a ticker-tape parade.

Eventually, I got better at making the trip, but Allison was more than happy to commute to Yonkers, so we alternated. By "alternated" I mean that she came to me roughly 90% of the time. And that was okay because, while for me driving is a torturous exercise filled with anxiety, Allison had been driving since the age of sixteen. For her, getting into a car was like slipping on a comfortable pair of shoes. In addition, she has the remarkable ability to go somewhere once and remember how to get there.

I continued to drive, however, but was never completely comfortable about getting around. I managed my anxiety until the time finally came when I didn't.

I was leaving a meeting in rural Connecticut. I had driven up in daylight and, beyond my normal nervousness about driving to places I'd never been to, I'd arrived mostly unscathed. When it was time to leave, it was dark, and I could not see the street signs on the few streets that had street signs. It wasn't long before I was completely lost. I panicked and called Allison. She somehow talked me onto the Hutchinson River Parkway and I finally made it home.

I knew I needed to fix this. I tried using Google Maps and Waze, but they're not infallible. At those times, I'd pull into the nearest gas station and ask Bob for directions. None of these were great solutions, but then I realized I had a secret weapon.

I always travel with Allison.

My Dentist Has a Brand New Inground Pool- Thanks to Me

There are enough people caring for my teeth to make up the starting five of a basketball team. My current "tooth team" consists of a periodontist, an endodontist, an oral surgeon, a general dentist, and a hygienist.

I spent the better part of my life neglecting my teeth. I didn't even know what dental floss was. I had the occasional cavity and even had a couple of teeth pulled but for the most part, I was lucky.

But when I hit my late forties, the pain was too frequent and intense to ignore. Based on a friend's recommendation, I went to see a dentist in the posh neighborhood of Manhattan's Upper East Side. Once inside, however, I thought I stepped into the lair of a forty-year-old who lived in his mother's basement. I did my best to ignore the ratty accordion doors and the torn leather couches and chose to conclude that despite the address, the doctor was unpretentious. After a thorough workup, he concluded I needed massive work on my gums before he could even begin to work on the disaster that my teeth had become, and as such, he had to introduce me to the wonderful world of root canals. Beyond the months of pain that awaited me was the cost. When Dr. X told me the price tag on my good dental health, I went into a state of shock. It was two-thirds of what I had paid for the co-op I lived in.

"Just think of this as if you're buying a car," the dentist said.

"I don't know what you drive but this is—I think—the cost of my next 3 cars," I replied.

My girlfriend had been urging me to see her dentist in suburban New Jersey. While I had no desire to go to New Jersey, I finally agreed see Dr. G, hoping to hear that my choice was to enjoy my current lifestyle with no teeth or accept a life of being homeless with a full set of choppers. The bad news was that the first dentist had been right—my teeth and gums were a mess and things would only get worse. The not-so-bad news was not having a Park Avenue dentist was going to save me a lot of money. Not that it would be cheap by any means.

I decided to commit to the dental work needed to keep whatever teeth I could before it was too late.

Thus, began four gum surgeries and a round of root canals before we could begin to visit the land of bridges and crowns. Three years and the cost of a Toyota Camry later, I finally had healthy gums and teeth. I dutifully had my teeth cleaned every three months and flossed regularly. So, I was finished with expensive dental surgery forever?

Wrong. Two years later my teeth rebelled. Again. The pain came out of nowhere. Nasty infections appeared on my gums, and I was once again on the road to agony and destitution.

The next phase of my dental odyssey? Implants! I needed two. Each took eighteen months, and each one made a huge dent in my meager savings.

Was I done yet? Nope. I soon learned that the same way household appliances break down, dental "appliances" like implants can, as well. In my case, this resulted in an actual conversation I had with my dentist's receptionist:

Elissa: Hello, Dr. Gruber's office.

Me: Hi, this is Ed Friedman. I'm a patient...

Elissa: Oh, hi Ed, what's up?

Me: Well, it seems that one of my implants has fallen out.

Elissa: You mean the crown came out?

Me: No. I mean the whole implant just fell out of my mouth.

Elissa: Wait. What were you eating?

Me: Well, the last thing I ate was a panini.

Elissa: Your whole implant fell out while you were eating a panini?

Me: Well not exactly. I was eating a panini Saturday evening and the tooth felt a little loose. Then in the middle of the night, the whole tooth just fell out of my mouth.

Elissa: What were you doing?

Me: I was sleeping.

Elissa: Wait. You were sleeping and the whole implant just fell out of your mouth?

Me: Yup

Elissa: Are you in any pain?

Me: No

Elissa: Is there any bleeding?

Me: No.

Elissa: It just fell out.

Me: Yeah

Elissa: You're sure it's the whole implant.

Me: I'm looking at it as we speak.

Elissa: I have to speak to the doctor. I'll call you back.

When I arrived at Dr. Gruber's office two days later, I couldn't shake the feeling that his office staff thought I had made this story up. I guess they thought it was just too weird to be true. I wish I had made it up. I certainly would have made it more interesting. ("Yeah, I was part of a Strongman competition, and I was pulling a Ford F-150 with my teeth, and dang it, the implant came out.") No fewer than six people plus the office manager asked if what they had heard about my gravity-defying implant was true. I suppose this is what passes for hot gossip at a dentist's office.

Of course, I needed a new implant, which meant yet another hit to my bank account.

I briefly considered what I could get for one of my kidneys on the black market, but that would just be trading one body part for another.

So, I bit the bullet (pun intended), and now my teeth are fine. I can chew whatever I want. So, I'm happy to go to dinner at any time.

But you'll have to pick me up.

I sold my car.

Turnpike Blues

In my ongoing quest to be a dutiful husband, I recently volunteered to drive my wife Allison from our home in New Rochelle New York to Newark Airport. I am a "white knuckle" driver with a terrible sense of direction. I hate driving and only do so when I absolutely must. But rather than make her take a taxi, I decided to brave the George Washington Bridge and deliver Allison to the airport myself.

Actually, Allison drove herself to the airport, as she knows how I feel about driving and is extremely comfortable behind the wheel. On the way there she pointed out the landmarks which would guide me back to New Rochelle on the trip back.

"Don't forget," she said, "when you leave the airport, look for the signs for 78 EAST." She repeated this many times, which I then chanted back at her as if I were a cult member. We arrived at the airport without incident, and I began my journey home.

I followed Allison's directions which I could now repeat like a Catholic schoolboy reciting his catechism. I made it onto 78 EAST. Given that it was mid-day and there was barely any traffic, I expected to be home in less than an hour. "Call me when you get home," Allison had instructed. "I'll probably still be waiting to board."

I had driven fewer than ten minutes and was about a hundred yards from the turnpike toll booth when I heard a loud pop. Followed by the unmistakable thump of a tire going flat. The hideous sounds of the rims hitting the highway surface almost drowned out my cursing. A median strip separating two lanes of traffic was within reach. I stopped there and thought about my options. Getting out of the car was clearly not one of them. Given the speed of the traffic rocketing past me, I was unlikely to make it to the side of the road without becoming a human pancake.

Luckily, I was prepared. Not to change the tire-I'm hopeless at that. But I knew how to call AAA. After being put on hold and told repeatedly how important my call was, I sat and watched the cars whiz by on either side of me. When an AAA representative finally came on, she told me that AAA could not enter the Turnpike for service because it was the domain of the New Jersey Turnpike Authority. But she would let the Authority know about my problem and they would send someone along soon to help me.

Thirty minutes later, a Turnpike Authority repair truck pulled up behind me and I leaped out of my car to meet him.

Stay in your car," the driver told me sternly.

Chastened, I got back in the car.

He changed the tire and then approached the window of my car to say, "This spare will not get you home." He gave me directions to a used tire place in Jersey City, which was only two exits away. So off I went. For about five minutes. At which point, I heard the spare blow out and wondered if I could cry and drive at the same time.

I rode the rim for another five minutes before arriving at another toll plaza where I was able to pull into the small employee parking lot. At least I was off the highway and could get out of the car.

Once again, I called AAA figuring that because I was off the highway, they could help me. I figured wrong. The AAA operator told me that the toll plaza is *also* under the jurisdiction of the Turnpike Authority, so I had to wait for them again. But this time they would send a flatbed truck.

Allison would be boarding soon. I now had a decision to make: if I called my wife before she got on the plane, she'd worry about how I was going to manage to extricate myself from this mess; and if I didn't call her, she'd worry all the way to Phoenix about what had happened to me.

I phoned her. Allison was concerned, but I put on my best "there's nothing to worry about" act, and mercifully, since the plane was about to take off, we had to cut our conversation short. At least she wouldn't worry - or so I thought.

The tow truck finally arrived, loaded my car on the flatbed, and brought me to a garage which, the driver assured me, would fix me up with a tire. They offloaded my car, with me in it, onto the street in front of the garage. I was close to my automotive problems being solved!

While I waited for the folks at the garage to get around to fixing my car, I sat in the only chair in the garage "office." A small, grubby room, decorated with posters for motor oil and a calendar from 2015. When I looked down at my phone, there were two voice mails. One was from Allison's business associate, Linda. Linda had never called me before, and I could not imagine why she would now. It turned out that Allison had asked her to find out how I was, and then text her. So much for my efforts to keep Allison from worrying. The other voicemail was from my office manager, deputized to find out what the hell had happened to me. I was supposed to have been back at my desk two hours ago. Since, at that point the staff was scattered over five counties and two states, I have no idea what they would have done if something had happened to me. But the thought was nice. I returned the calls and reassured everyone that I was off the highway, safe and that I would be home soon.

Eventually, the mechanic put a full-size tire on the car. At that point, I was so paranoid about another blowout that I bought another full-sized tire and threw it in the trunk, just in case.

Now I was ready to go home. I could see the entrance to the highway fifty feet away from the shop. I was optimistic. There it was in big letters-Route 78, so I got on the highway. However, it wasn't long before I realized I was headed in the wrong direction. This was confirmed by the fact that I should have been driving toward the George Washington Bridge, but was, in fact, driving away from it. Once again, I got off the turnpike.

I consulted Google Maps, which led to my driving around Jersey City for the next 20 minutes until I made a random right turn into what looked like a dead-end. Instead, at last, I found the entrance to Route 78 *East*. Now I simply had to drive home from New Jersey in the middle of rush hour. Given the way my day had gone so far, I was afraid another vehicular mishap would befall me. But I arrived back in New Rochelle with all parts of the car intact and pulled into the garage of our apartment building.

I got out of my car. But before I left the garage to go into the building, I looked back and said to my Toyota, "I hope you're happy here, cause I'm not moving you again, ever."

Section Two: **THINGS THAT COULD HAVE HAPPENED**

A Wish Come True

For years I struggled to maintain a healthy weight and control my high blood pressure and cholesterol. My life was full of medication, diets, and boring exercise.

Now, I wake up every day knowing the world is my oyster… hot fudge sundae…or French fries. That's because I have the unique superpower to eat whatever I want, in whatever quantity I want, without having any negative consequences for my health while at the same time being enriched by the food's nutrients---negligible, in some cases as they may be.

The medical establishment has not been able to explain this condition or discover its origin. The discovery of this nameless affliction(?) took place six months after a particularly painful breakup during which I self-medicated with enormous amounts of the kinds of food I had previously been denying myself. I had not stepped on a scale during that time and had given up any form of exercise, preferring to binge-watch revenge-themed action movies and mindlessly eat Pringles. Appearing for my annual physical I was completely prepared for spiked cholesterol, elevated blood pressure, and a stern lecture from my doctor. When she informed me that my blood tests were fine and my weight hadn't changed, I left her office in a state of confusion.

Three months later, continuing my pattern of gluttony and sloth, I repeated the blood tests. Nothing had changed. My doctor, at first skeptical, sent me for a battery of new, more sophisticated tests. These too yielded no information.

I now walk around in a state of near delirium with the knowledge that I don't have to think about the consequences of what I'm eating. I can simply indulge in whatever culinary whim occurs to me.

Before I acquired this power, my concern over cholesterol, high blood pressure and heart disease would find me sitting in a restaurant and opting for salads, while I would see someone at a nearby table indulging in a mound of mashed potatoes and pork chops slathered in gravy. My unrequited yearnings only increased when I watched television and would see the ubiquitous presentations of stuffed tacos, pizza, Big Macs, and Whoppers. Now I can abandon all concern and sit in front of the television with my half gallon of Edy's fudge ripple and eat it until my arm gets too tired to lift the spoon.

What has become inconvenient to explain is the protective detail parked outside my door and with me wherever I go. Apparently, our government has been made aware that the Chinese government is planning to kidnap me in order to conduct experiments on my body to find out the cause of my condition. They want to replicate my physiology and monetize it. Our elected officials are doing anything they can to prevent that. As you would expect, if anyone is going to make money off of this it will be their donors, Big Pharma.

My only problem occurs when I'm with other people. Eating at restaurants with my health-conscious friends has become embarrassing. I can detect a thinly veiled anger at my ordering without concern for caloric content. I must admit that I have felt it necessary to order broiled fish (no butter) on occasion just to make everyone feel better. In my more selfish or indulgent moods, I don't grapple with the decision of whether to have the tiramisu or the pie ala mode. I simply order both. Everyone around the table will sigh. Do they hate me? Maybe.

But I can live with that.

As long as there's bacon.

I'm Calling B.S.

Are you tired of trying to decipher the double-talk or outright lies from:

Auto mechanics?

Car salesmen?

Real estate agents?

Government officials?

And everyone else who won't give you a straight answer?

We've got the solution. It's the BULLSHIT INDICATOR APP

Designed by Mean Girl Avengers, this app uses the latest in Russian bot technology and is compatible with Apple and Android phones. It's simple to use and unobtrusive. You just record the person giving you what might be questionable information. As long as the phone mic is within five feet of the speaker's voice, it will pick up what they're saying and give you the information you need.

Say you've brought your car in for yearly inspection. When you come to pick up the car, the mechanic ushers you into the office. You know this will not be good news, so you activate the BULLSHIT INDICATOR APP. When the mechanic tells you your car needs repairs on some part of the car you couldn't identify with a gun to your head, just say, "I have to think about it," and step away for a minute. If you see a green light on your phone, you can be confident that you're not being lied to. On the other hand, if your phone flashes a red BULLSHIT sign, go back to the mechanic, pay for the inspection, say "no thanks" and go out to find another (hopefully less corrupt) service station. If they had gotten away with this scam, they would have pulled the same thing every year. You will have saved yourself thousands of dollars.

The BULLSHIT INDICATOR APP will also come in handy for house-hunting. When you're walking through a potential new home and the real estate agent says, "We've got many offers over the asking price," The BULLSHIT INDICATOR APP alert will tell you that you don't have to make a ridiculously high offer to purchase this home. Or suppose you hear something like "Oh that ceiling discoloration? That's nothing." With your BULLSHIT INDICATOR APP already activated, you'll know instantly that there is not only water damage but possibly asbestos. Make your way out of there as fast as possible, but memorize the agent's name for future avoidance.

What about day-to-day personal interactions? The BULLSHIT INDICATOR APP also works for when a sister-in-law claims she can't come to your Tupperware party because she has a cold and doesn't want to make everyone sick; or a spouse saying for the fourth time that month, they have to work late.

And of course, you'll save countless hours not waiting and constantly checking your phone. The BULLSHIT INDICATOR APP has an audio feature that registers phone calls. So when a doctor's office, contractor, or potential client says they'll get right back to you, and you hear three short beeps, you might as well go run some errands or catch up on your Netflix waiting list. You aren't getting that call anytime soon.

The BULLSHIT INDICATOR APP is effective across cable and airwaves. If you're watching a political speech or debate, you simply turn on the app and hold it in front of the television or computer. However, use the app judiciously for these events. It's likely to overload.

Job Posting/Employment Application
Position: Assassin

Justice-seeking organization is looking for an experienced individual to carry out sub-contracts.

The successful applicant will:

- have completed a minimum of twenty confirmed contracts.
- be fluent in at least one language besides English.
- have no outstanding warrants.

Compensation

Commensurate with experience

While this is not a full-time salaried position, the successful applicant will have fully paid medical benefits, dental and vision, including coverage for elective plastic surgery and fingerprint removal.

We are an equal opportunity employer committed to diversity, equity, and inclusion.

IF INTERESTED IN APPLYING, PLEASE COMPLETE THE FOLLOWING:

Name: (Please include all aliases and code names.)

Address: (Please include all safe houses and homes of significant partners, marital or otherwise.)

Phone number: (Please include ALL cell phones as well as active burners.)

Email: (Please list all active accounts.)

Date of Birth: (Please list one for each alias.)

Social Security Number(s):

How did you hear about this opportunity? (Please list names and aliases of whoever let you know that we have an opening. Note: Individual in question must be alive and fully conscious.)

References: (List three living people who will vouch for your work.)

Please indicate all methods of carrying out contracts for which you have expertise. (Check all that apply.)

High powered rifle _____
.45 caliber revolver _____
Garotte _____
Knife _____
C-4 _____
Baseball bat _____
Poison _____
Flame Thrower _____
Chain Saw _____
Bare hands _____
Other (please specify)

_____

Which is your <u>preferred</u> method for carrying out contracts?

(Indicate your two top methods.)

Why do you want to work with our firm?

More travel _____
Less travel _____
More important targets _____
Access to our state-of-the-art weaponry _____
Elite lawyers on retainer _____

Why did you leave your last employer?

They are all incarcerated _____
They are all dead _____
They didn't pay you so you killed them _____
No opportunity for advancement _____

Attach your resume.

(List targets, locations, dates of completion.)

What kind of salary are you looking for?

Monthly retainer _____
Per target _____

What salary will you settle for and not kill us?

Monthly retainer _____
Per target _____

What is your blood type? (We want to make sure we have an adequate supply.)

Are you missing any:
internal organs _____
limbs _____
digits _____
other _____

Date available
Do you have any pending contracts? If so, can you get a sub?

Are you a U.S. citizen? (Not that we care.)

List passports (real or fake) you currently hold?

Education

What's the highest level you completed? (actual) __

Special skills (besides the obvious)

Juggling _____

Gourmet Cooking _____

Horseback riding _____

Swimming _____

Unicycle _____

Other _____

Languages spoken

Is there anyone in your life you'd be concerned about, should they be kidnapped, killed, or held for ransom? (Indicate name, relationship, home address.)

Please leave your completed application under the door of ACME Exterminating Company between 3:00 and 6:00 A.M.

Peach and Blueberry Cobbler

Annotated for the baking-challenged and heartbroken

Makes 4 to 6 servings.

Not a chance. At least not while I'm using food to fill the emotional hole in my life after my girlfriend Gloria of three years dumped me. I'll be lucky if I don't eat the whole thing.

1 stick (8 tablespoons) butter

Any illusion about this dessert not being terrible for me is smashed right off the bat. Considering what else I'm doing to self-sabotage, this is the least of it.

1 cup all-purpose flour, spooned into the cup and leveled off

OK I can do that. I only hope that when I've completed this step, I don't look like a second grader after erasing the blackboard.

2 teaspoons baking powder

Do I even have baking powder? God knows that Gloria never baked me a cake or anything else. I hated the Costco birthday cake she would get me. Not to mention the fact that she always spelled my name wrong.

½ teaspoon fine salt

I know I have salt. At least she didn't pour it directly into my wounds.

2/3 cup granulated sugar

I don't have sugar. When Gloria left me, she left nothing that was sweet. I do have Splenda. That's all I have left now that she's gone-artificial sweetness.

1 cup whole milk

Who uses whole milk anymore? Oh, that's right she did. When I once suggested that one percent would be healthier, she said, "Stop being such a baby."

1 large egg

Well I have an egg. Is it large? How the hell would I know? I'll probably have to crack it open-just like she did to my heart.

1 teaspoon vanilla extract

This little dark bottle looks like it could be vanilla extract. I can't read the label. It looks as if it's been here for a long time. It was probably here before she moved in. I can't believe that random bottle of vanilla extract lasted longer than the relationship.

3 cups ½-inch slices firm-ripe unpeeled peaches (3 or 4 medium peaches)

Oh man! I only have two peaches. Guess I need to go to the supermarket. The silver lining is that I can bring home what I bought and not be told that everything I got was wrong.

1 cup blueberries

I haven't got blueberries either. Clearly, I have not thought this project through. Well, what can I expect? I'm currently wearing two left shoes.

Spiced sugar topping: 1 tablespoon granulated sugar mixed with ¼ teaspoon each ground cinnamon and nutmeg and a pinch of allspice.

OK. I can find the sugar, cinnamon, and nutmeg, but what the hell is allspice?

(90 minutes and a trip to the supermarket later)

I made the mistake of asking a fellow shopper about allspice. She assumed I was trying to pick her up. So, I asked a guy and I got the same response. Screw the allspice. Whatever it is I'm doing without it.

Okay, everything else is here. I can start.

Preheat the oven to 350°F.

Despite Gloria constantly complaining about how worthless I am in the kitchen; I actually know how to do this.

Put the stick of butter in a 10-inch cast-iron skillet that's 2 inches deep.

This skillet is more than 2 inches deep. Is it cast iron? I have no idea. All I know is that if she hit me in the face with this skillet it would have hurt less than what she did.

Place the skillet in the oven and melt the butter until golden brown, 13 to 16 minutes, watching carefully after about 10 minutes.

I knew I shouldn't have turned on the game. The absence of being yelled at because I was watching the game was so wonderful that I forgot what I was doing. Is the butter supposed to be this dark?

Remove the skillet from the oven.

OwOwOwOwOw. I have to remember to get potholders. She must have taken them all. Yet another way to burn me.

Meanwhile, in a large bowl, whisk together the flour, baking powder, salt, and sugar.

Whisk? I thought whisk was a detergent. I just looked it up on Amazon and saw fourteen different whisks. I don't have any of them, so I'm using a fork.

Measure the milk in a glass measure, break in the egg, add the vanilla, and beat with a fork until blended.

So, I can use a fork. Hah! Good call on my part, canceling the Amazon whisk order.

Pour into the flour mixture and whisk until smooth.

Fuck the whisk. I'm using a fork.

Pour the batter into the hot butter in the skillet. Do not stir; the butter may rise to the top, which is not a problem.

Thanks for telling me it's not a problem. Like that would ever have occurred to me.

Arrange some of the peaches on the batter in a tight circle around the inside of the pan and pile the rest in the center.

Yeah, this doesn't look right. It looks less like a cake than a fourth grade science project that I dropped running for the bus.

Scatter the blueberries on top.

Okay, scattering, I can do.

Sprinkle with the spiced sugar topping.

That's not happening.

Bake the cobbler until golden, the fruit is tender and bubbly, and a toothpick inserted into the cake comes out clean, 30 to 35 minutes.

Kinda looks like a third-grade science project that didn't get a good grade. Oh, God, she's right. I'm hopeless.

Transfer to a wire rack and serve warm or at room temperature, maybe with a scoop of vanilla ice cream.

Hey, this isn't too bad. if you ignore the fact that it's ugly. No problem. I can eat it with my eyes closed.

If there are leftovers, remove them from the skillet to a plate.

Hah! If only. Not gonna happen.

That was actually good. I'm a better baker than I thought I was.

Now I'm ready for something more ambitious. Bouillabaisse? Chicken cordon bleu? Paella?

As long as it doesn't need allspice.

I Will Not Be Ignored

September 2, 2020

Wilson Adams
c/o The Write Place

Dear Mr. Adams:

I am writing to express my appreciation for your seminar, "Mastering Flash Fiction."

I'm sure I can speak for the other attendees of your seminar when I say that the wisdom you imparted was both informative and inspirational. I've been looking at all my previous writing through the lens of that wisdom.

You may be interested (but not surprised, I'm sure) to know that I gave your seminar an excellent recommendation on Yelp.

It was most kind of you to offer to read the work of seminar participants. In response, I have attached my most recent attempt at short fiction. I'm sure the piece will benefit from your insight.

Of course, I realize you have many demands on your time, so I'm not expecting an immediate response.

With gratitude,

Nathan Remson

October 16, 2020

Dear Mr. Adams:

I just thought I would follow up on my email of September 2nd to which I'd attached a short story in response to your generous offer to review the work of seminar participants and provide feedback. I realize that you must be quite busy, but I wanted to make sure you received my email. I really don't mean to bother you. I just thought it was responsible of me to check in with you.

All the best,

Nathan Remson

November 23, 2020

Dear Mr. Adams:

It seems you have not received either of my emails. I am wondering if you regularly check your Spam folder. It has been my experience that, on occasion, important messages are routed incorrectly and wind up in Spam. I am hoping that has occurred here, and you will be able to easily locate my email and attached short story which you so generously offered to critique.

Wishing you a peaceful holiday season

Nathan Remson

January 7, 2021

Mr. Adams:

I trust you had an enjoyable holiday and are no doubt digging out from under the many requests for your attention you've received during this period. In the spirit of "first come, first served," I would like to remind you of my original email to you on September 2 of last year. Just to jog your memory, I responded to your generous offer of critiquing the work of attendees of your seminar "Mastering Flash Fiction."

I am writing to remind you that it has been four months since I responded.

If you've had second thoughts about your offer, I would appreciate the courtesy of a reply so I can seek feedback elsewhere.

Nathan Remson

February 2, 2021

Mr. Adams:

I can only assume that for reasons known only to yourself you have been deleting my emails as you receive them. This means, of course, that you will not read this email either. Having said that, the only reason this communication exists is for me to cathartically express my disappointment in having a prize (the benefit of your expertise) dangled in front of me and then cruelly snatched away without any explanation. This, sir, is bad form. And also, if your beliefs run in this direction, very bad karma. Mainly, it's just rude.

I now find myself in the unenviable position of looking at your work in a new light. I must place you among people like Ernest Hemingway,

Woody Allen, Ezra Pound, Mel Gibson, and Richard Wagner--revered artists, but far less successful human beings.

Disillusioned and Disappointed,

Nathan Remson

June 6, 2021

Mr. Adams

It has been nine months since my first email in response to your offer of a critique of the work of seminar attendees. Let me remind you that no one asked you to make this offer. It was not part of the seminar's advertised benefits. You offered it of your own volition. So, if you're harboring any feelings about being "put upon," let me suggest that you place the blame for that right back on yourself.

On looking back over my notes from the seminar I realize that fully half of the "wisdom" you imparted to us was things I already knew. In the ensuing months, I have uncovered many websites with free classes where I have found half of the remaining fifty percent of the knowledge you imparted. Not to be ungrateful, I will credit you for the remaining twenty-five percent, which was new to me and not to be found online. With that in mind, I feel compelled to ask you to please send me a seventy-five percent refund. If you don't, I will edit my previous five-star review to reflect my current reassessment of the effectiveness (or lack thereof) of the seminar.

I have also used this time to obtain copies of your collections. Thankfully, they were available at my public library as I have no interest in throwing good money after bad. Upon reading your stories, I found myself questioning why on earth I would take writing advice from you.

You are a terrible writer and an even worse human being.

Nathan Remson

July 5, 2021

Dear Nathan

I truly apologize for this long-overdue response to the request for my input on the short story that you sent me last September. I was so happy to hear how much you learned from our time together at the seminar.

My lack of response to your letter was due to an unfortunate water-skiing accident that befell me last Labor Day. I have been in an induced coma for the past nine months and it was only last week that my brain functions have progressed to the point that I can read and write. I have just begun to review my emails, and I was so happy to receive yours.

As you might expect, I have a lot to catch up on. This note is just to let you know that I'll be happy to review the work you sent me. Can't wait to read it.

Gratefully,

Wilson Adams

I'm Dying to Know If I'm Dying

Sitting in this drab gray room with nothing to look at but posters of the digestive tract, and illustrations of every possible gut-related ailment known to man, I await the diagnosis that will determine my future.

I'm not thinking about what I'll do if the news is good. What's the point of that? I'm not one of these people who, after hearing good news, will have some epiphany about making the most out of every day. I had no desire to climb Macchu Pichu before I got sick, so why would I want to do it now? No, good news will simply send me home to continue to enjoy the pleasant but unadventurous small pleasures I can without risking my life.

And to wait for the next medical crisis.

No, it's far more important that I prepare for the bad news. Is my will up to date? Are my health care directives in place? Does my health care proxy state what should happen if I can't make decisions? And when should I start giving away my stuff?

Most important—Before I die, I've got to remember to clear my browsing history! Whoever inherits my computer doesn't need to know about my visits to mudwrestlinghoneys.com. Maybe I should just toss my laptop in the Hudson River.

I never realized how much work it is to die.

Of course, if I drop dead here and now, I won't have to worry about any of this. But that's not going to happen. With my luck, my end will be a gradual deterioration, which I can only hope will be accompanied by lots and lots of very effective pain medication, and people looking at me with sad, loving eyes--fewer and fewer of them as I get closer to death, until, finally, the small group of family and friends who are at my bedside give me "permission to let go."

Regrets? At my age, if I really wanted to do something, I would have done it by now. Anything I didn't do was due to fear or laziness, not lack of opportunity.

What do I leave behind? Not much. I have no children. My siblings are scattered around the country and truth be told we're not very close.

My friends will probably hold a memorial service for me at which I'll be presented in a positive light because that's what social protocol demands. Not that it will be tough to say nice things about me. I'm a nice guy. But what importance did my life have? There won't be a New York Times obit giving me credit for some significant achievement. Just a small group of people saying things like "he was a really good listener," or "he was always supportive of his friends" Nobody's life will be altered by my going. Maybe that's sad, but at least my death will leave no one devastated.

Once you're dead your problems may be over--but it's monumentally inconvenient for the survivors. A few poor souls will have to sort through my stuff, clean out my apartment, and meet with my lawyer. At least a few friends and loved ones will reap a smidgen of financial benefit.

The silver lining about not dying wealthy is I don't have enough assets so that people will fight over them.

I guess if the news is bad, I'm going to have to tell people. Whom do I tell first? And what do I tell them? Maybe I can just post this on Facebook?

"Hi everyone. If I miss wishing you a happy birthday, don't be offended. It's just that I've got six months to live and I'm in pretty bad shape."

Even I know that's a little over the top. But it's easier than having to tell the same sad story over and over. That's no way to spend your last precious days on earth.

If I'm dying, I shouldn't have to spend the little time I have left putting myself through that kind of ordeal. Or enduring conversations where people ask me If I've tried some plant grown in the jungles of Bolivia or Croatia or listen to well-intentioned but meaningless offers to "call if you need anything." This means I have to call and ask for help. Anyone who knows anything about me knows that's not going to happen.

I know! I'll write a letter.

Dear friends and family and anyone else who still may give a hoot. Well, it looks like I'll be "giving up the ghost"; "buying the farm," "taking a dirt nap" or whatever euphemism you like best. I've got about six months to live, but the doctor tells me I'll stop making sense after four. So, if you choose to say goodbye any time after that, please don't be offended if I think you're Abraham Lincoln.

Some of you may believe I owe you an apology for something I did or said some years ago, about which I have absolutely no recollection. If you hadn't brought it up until now it couldn't have been that big a deal. Just suck it up. Some of you may think you owe me an apology for some hurt you inflicted on me. Too late. Take it to your grave/priest/shrink. I don't want to hear it.

Speaking of things I don't want to hear, the doctor just came into the room.

She's smiling.

I guess I will make my co-pay after all.

Job Posting: Chief of Staff for Member of U.S. Senate

Under the direction of absolutely no one, the Chief of Staff's responsibilities include creating plausible deniability scenarios for situations including, but not limited to, obfuscating extramarital affairs, covering up illegal stock trades, and hiding the domestic employment of undocumented immigrants. Additional responsibilities include paying operatives to discover compromising information on rivals, and inventing said information if none can be discovered.

The selected candidate will also oversee the Senator's staff. These duties include, but are not limited to:

Supervising the Press Secretary, including vetting the content of all press releases, communications, photo ops and briefings, and throwing them under the bus when they make an error.

Overseeing Constituent Services, which is the Senator's connection to their public, and where constituents with problems can come and seek the Senator's help. The successful candidate for the Chief of Staff position must ensure that no staffer agrees to or promises anything to anyone, ever.

Tracking the Senator's polling numbers, revealing them when they trend upward and burying them when they nosedive.

Overseeing the re-election campaign staff, including administering corporal punishment for anyone uttering the name of the Senator's primary or general election opponent.

Qualifications

The candidate must have:

Excellent speaking skills, including experience with intimidation strategies, and the ability to deliver half-truths in both press conferences and interviews and sarcastic remarks when asked about the rival party. Ability to disguise one's voice on the telephone a plus.

Willingness to act on explicit instructions without question.

Willingness to commit perjury to protect the reputation of the Senator.

Black belt in Tae Kwan Do.

Voted (in his or her own name) in every election for which a vote could be cast.

Had fingerprints medically removed.

No (obvious) connection to any international crimes, as extensive international travel is required.

No past video, photographic or social media evidence of any racist, homophobic, or antisemitic behavior (scrubbed or not scrubbed).

No criminal record whatsoever (even expunged).

No affiliation with any political, or activist group or at least none that can be traced back to them.

No moral center.

Benefits

Enormous salary.

International travel on "fact-finding" missions.

High-quality health care as the selected candidate is allowed zero sick days.

Unlimited discretionary budget for miscellaneous expenses (no reports required).

This is a high-profile, sensitive position that calls for discretion,

judgment, and the ability to think quickly. The successful candidate will be on call 24/7 and have no discernible personal life. Deceased parents a plus. At times the Chief of Staff will be asked to escort an unnamed (in the interest of national security) person to public events. A willingness to sign a non-disclosure agreement is mandatory.

Looking for a home? Zillow Will Tell You Everything You Need to Know…and Less

The proliferation of websites with real estate listings has empowered everyday people (uninformed individuals) to act as their own real estate agents. While I applaud having information accessible to all, the veracity of this information is open to serious doubt. Many times, people marketing real estate, while not exactly crossing the line to untruth, bang hard right against it. In my own search for a place to live I came across the following listings on the internet. What I found on the in-person examination diverged from my expectations.

1st Floor 2BR Condo in The Gardens awaits your final touches to make this home your own! Bus stop right outside the complex and the Metro North Hudson line only 20 minutes to NYC. Just 5 minutes to downtown and all it has to offer, from restaurants, shops, and parks, to museums, *theatres, and a shopping center. Easy access to major highways. Must be owner-occupied for a period of 5 years before renting is allowable. Complex offers unassigned parking for a yearly fee of $150.*

How I'd describe it after I saw it:

If you live here, you can use your creativity to decorate the bars on the windows of this first-floor unit. Bus fumes will force you to keep your windows closed at all times. However, this does help to keep the rat population down to manageable levels. Proximity to the city and its attractions is a great feature, as you don't want to spend any more time in this unit than necessary. The parking fee is very reasonable, if you don't include the Uber fees you'll pay to get to and from a parking space, invariably no closer than a mile from the unit. The five-year rental restriction is not much of an issue as it is unlikely you can stand to live there for more than two.

Sunny bright one-bedroom w/office/nursery in a well-maintained complex. Assigned parking and storage. Updated kitchen and bath as well as new flooring and paint. Wall of closets in the bedroom with one cedar closet. Heat lamp in bathroom. A large balcony and third-floor location make this unit special with more living space and privacy. The complex has an outdoor pool for summer fun. Great for a starter home or downsizing.

How I'd describe it after I saw it:

You'll likely have to install blackout curtains as this unit has both eastern and western exposures. Maintenance staff live in the complex, but good luck finding them to fix anything. The storage unit is large enough to fit a birdcage and two rolls of aluminum foil. The heat lamp is essential as the bathroom is unheated--except in summer. The balcony is currently supported by Legos.

Lovely, light-filled, pet-friendly, Westville PO condominium with assigned parking is just what you've been looking for! Primary bedroom with en-suite bath, 2nd large bedroom, and hall bath. Kitchen with stainless steel appliances. Freshly painted with gleaming hardwood floors, 57sf private balcony, private storage, and a common barbeque/picnic area. Common laundry in the building. A short walk to the village, Metro North, parks, shops, and restaurants.

How I'd describe it after I saw it:

PO designation is a tipoff that this condo is at the edge of the sketchy part of town. Your parking space is right in front of the unit, which is important as you'll likely have to run into your unit from the car to avoid being shot. In this case, "stainless steel appliances" just means the previous tenants removed the stains from the surfaces of the refrigerator and the stove (both decades old). The condo is indeed pet-friendly in that whatever pet you have will be vigorously humped by every other pet in the complex. That the unit is downwind from the common barbecue area means you won't smell the burnt flesh coming from the sacrificing of small animals.

Welcome to serenity at its best. Living in this condo is like being on vacation every day, starting with the breathtaking Hudson River Views. This renovated unit is just what you've been looking for and includes a modern kitchen with stainless steel appliances and granite countertops, new floors in the living room/dining area and two new bathrooms as well. You won't have a problem with storage as this unit has excellent closet space. Step onto your private balcony to sip your morning coffee, relax in the primary bedroom, which offers a great breeze, or look beyond the front door for a woodland view of the Croton Aqueduct Trail. The complex offers a recently renovated lobby, a pool, a gym, covered parking, storage, and a bike room. You couldn't ask for a more convenient location. Please verify all info.

How I'd describe it after I saw it:

Yes, you've got a great view of the Hudson from the kitchen window…if you manage to contort your body to a 45-degree angle. Renovated, in this case, means they've patched the bullet holes, painted, and replaced the windows that were broken in an alcohol-fueled screaming fight between the previous tenants. There is no problem with storage unless you have more than two file boxes of things you'd like to put away. If that's not the case, you can pay an exorbitant fee to rent additional storage space. See, no problem. The pool is open year-round, but it's unheated, unchlorinated, and generally disgusting. The bike room exists as storage for the bikes stolen by the son of the superintendent. If you have a bike you want to hold on to, best you lug it up to your unit. And if none of this convinces you to run, "please verify all info" just tells you that everything you read before is bullshit.

Welcome to the Gateway. This 4 Bedroom 2 Bath split level Garden unit is a unique find. A combination of gleaming hardwood and parquet flooring flow throughout the upper and lower levels of this magnificent oversized 4 Bdrm 1900 sq ft home. The entry level offers an open concept that combines a formal dining room, living room, and eat-in kitchen with sliding glass doors that with just two steps up, open to a private patio. Upstairs find the primary bedroom with en-suite bath and lots of closet space. Three additional bedrooms with large closets offer the versatility to allow you to use one room as a home office, den, or family room. Enjoy the community's private pool and playground. This fabulous garden apartment is located near scenic parks. Minutes to the railroad for easy commuting.

How I'd describe it after I saw it:

This unit is unique in that it's the only one with a metropolis of termites underneath the hardwood floor. This will probably not be a problem for long, however, as the water table is less than a half inch below your floor. The first good rain should render the unit uninhabitable. I'd suggest flood insurance, but the insurance companies know about this so you won't be able to get any. I wouldn't count on using any of the spaces as a home office. The unit next door houses a Metallica cover band. They have gigs at night so your sleep will be undisturbed, but they rehearse all day long. Noise-canceling headphones will not help.

Rarely available, turnkey, luxuriously renovated sun-drenched two-bedroom two- bath Penthouse apartment in The Windchester, a doorman building all within walking distance to Metro North Train, shops, restaurants, & movie theater, & the Farmer's Market! A commuter's dream, this light, open, airy top floor apartment has sweeping views, features an open concept kitchen, custom built-ins and shades, a primary bedroom w/ private bath, a spacious second bedroom & generous closets & storage. The value of a renovated turnkey apt today is tremendous & this apartment has been thoroughly & tastefully redone: Quartz countertops/island, stainless steel appliances, designer bathrooms, custom Elfa walk-in closets, w/ all new electrical, plumbing & light fixtures. Tucked back from the road, this bldg features maintained grounds, elevator access, laundry room, storage units, and

on-site parking waitlist; outdoors $65, Garage $97. This diamond is a

rare offering not to be missed! (Building is non-smoking, no pets

allowed please!) Financial requirements: 25% Min Down Payment,

Min Credit Score of 700, 24 Months of Reserves Required, Max 30%

Debt-to-Income. All offers to include recently updated pre-approval or

proof of funds & completed co-op questionnaire.

How I'd describe it after I saw it:

It's rarely available because management has yet to figure out how to
get rid of the smell of the decomposed body discovered after three
months. The doorman, when he shows up, is usually drunk and can be
counted on to tell you that the package you expected was never
delivered. The sweeping views consist of a landfill and a soon-to-be-
completed office building that will obliterate any bit of daylight. The
"new" fixtures are new to this unit, but they have been buried in the
superintendent's storeroom for about a decade. Besides the financial
requirements, prospective tenants are required to donate a pint of blood

each year, submit to a complete medical examination, and sign a pledge not to have any children.

It may be fun to indulge in "real estate porn," but don't get your hopes up by what you see on your computer. In case this message has been too subtle… PEOPLE LIE. You'd be better served to get yourself a reputable real estate agent.

If you can find one.

Love at Worst Sight

As they walked along the path by the East River, both Rita and Joe were happy about how well this date was going. They had connected well on phone calls and on Zoom, but this was the first time they had met in person.

They stopped to look across the water to Roosevelt Island.

"I can't believe I've been in New York for eight months and hadn't tried Szechuan food," Joe remarked.

"I'm glad you tried it," said Rita. "And I'm really glad you liked it."

"I'm glad I tried it too." I must confess that I'm usually a little slow to try new things."

Rita had been looking for an opening to ask something she'd been wondering about. This was it.

"Have you been out with a Black woman before? "She asked

Joe looked at her quizzically. "Before what?"

"Before now."

"I'm not sure what you mean."

"OK let me try to put this another way. I'm just wondering. Do you date a lot of Black women? Or maybe it's a fantasy you're indulging?"

"I'm sorry but why we're talking about Black women?"

"Are you uncomfortable talking about race?"

"I don't think so. I haven't thought much about that question. I suppose not in the abstract, but there are probably circumstances where I'd feel uncomfortable."

"Is talking to me one of those circumstances?"

"Why would it be? It's really easy to talk to you. I just don't understand why we're talking about race."

"You think just because I'm out with a white man I don't identify as a Black woman?"

"I wasn't aware that you identify as a Black woman."

"Really? Look at me again."

Joe looks directly at Rita, struck by the smoothness of her skin and her expressive eyes.

"You're very attractive."

Rita's mouth opens but no sound comes out.

"I'm sorry," says Joe. "Am I missing something?"

"Look if this is some misguided diversity exercise, I'm not appreciating it!"

"Wait a minute" Joe responded, "Are you Black?"

"Of course. Isn't it obvious?"

"Not to me. There's something I haven't told you. I have

dyschromatopsia."

"You have what?"

"I can't distinguish skin color in other people."

"Wait...wait...So you're telling me when you look at people, you're...

"Colorblind."

"So, when you clicked on my profile you had no idea..."

"Nope"

"Wow. So, everybody looks white to you?"

"Actually, everybody looks kinda beige."

"And this has never come up when you dated before?"

"Nope, I'm from Duluth. It's pretty monochromatic out there."

"But you've been in New York for...what...eight months?"

"Yeah, but you know no one talks about race here. It's not even acknowledged. I just thought that everybody was incredibly sophisticated, and that New York was post-racial."

"Let me disabuse you of that notion. There is no such thing as post-racial."

"Well, that's disappointing."

"I don't think so. It's good to celebrate the things that make us unique and different...even if we all look beige to you."

"Sorry. I should have told you, but I didn't think it was relevant."

"You didn't even entertain the possibility that I wasn't white?" Rita asked.

"Well, after all, I did find you on a Jewish dating site."

"So, somebody Black can't be Jewish?" Rita snapped.

"Of course they can. I'm sorry to have offended you I was assuming based on a stereotype. I apologize."

"Don't," she said with a grin. I'm not Jewish."

"So, what were you doing on J Date."

"I just wanted to meet a Jewish guy. You know what they say. Jewish guys have a reputation for spoiling the women in their life."

"Yeah, I've heard that too."

"Wait are you trying to tell me you're not one of those Jewish guys who treat women well? You could have fooled me."

"No. I treat women very well, or at least I do my best. There haven't been any complaints...but...I'm not Jewish either."

"What?"

"I've never dated anyone Jewish. Since I came to New York I've dated a lot, but nothing's really worked out for me. I haven't clicked with anyone, and...you know... they say Jewish women motivate guys to be more successful. I'm not particularly ambitious, and I always thought if I had a little more drive, I'd get further…so …"

"You know I thought it was a little weird that you hadn't tried Schezuan food."

"I really do like *Fiddler on the Roof*, though."

"So, do I. Everybody likes *Fiddler on the Roof*. It's an iconic American musical. That doesn't make either of us Jews."

"Well, this didn't work out the way either of us expected," Rita said after a minute.

"Yes, but on the other hand, I've never had a date like this." Joe thought for a moment then continued. "OK. I don't know you well enough to know how you're feeling right now. Are you angry or sad? Did I do some 'white thing' that bothered you?"

Instead of answering, Rita reflected, "I've always hated people who were prejudiced, and just accepted stereotypes. Where's a mirror when you need one?"

"Can we get back to talking about you and me? Let's just think for a minute. There are lots of things we have in common that have nothing to do with race or religion."

"Right, we both hate Game of Thrones…"

"…but we like Shakespeare."

"We both hate camping …"

"We share the same politics …"

"…and it would be a deal-breaker for both of us if we didn't."

"We both moved away from home…"

"…but we both come back for the holidays."

"And we're both sick and tired of serial dating and want to meet someone we're compatible with."

"That's all great," said Rita, but I've got to be honest here and you need to be honest with me as well. We wouldn't have gotten this far unless I was physically attracted to you. I assume that's true for you as well. But you didn't know I was Black. Does knowing that affect how you see me?"

"The thing is," Joe said, "I can't "see" you any other way than I see you. I liked what I saw then, and I like what I see now."

"I like what I see too," Rita said.

"We still have a lot in common. We're still physically attracted to each other."

And we've both embarrassed ourselves," Rita said.

"So, we're way ahead of most people who have only had one date."

"What are you thinking?"

"I'm thinking, Joe replied, we should go on a second date."

"Yeah, let's do it. You want to try Mexican food next time? Do they have Mexican food in Duluth?

"Do Doritos count?"

"Oy vey."

Note Left Under the Door

To: my neighbor in the building

From: the woman in 3G

I just thought I'd take this moment to say thank you for using every washing machine in the laundry room at the same time. What an unexpected treat to see you commandeer all the washers. It's a testament to your managerial acumen that you could operate all six machines at once. I marvel at your ability to place quarters in all the slots. It must feel gratifying to have accomplished that. Watching you, I had this image of you in Las Vegas playing multiple slot machines simultaneously. Is that where you gained your experience? Maybe you could petition the landlord to equip the laundry room with blinking neon lights and loud music, and the super could come around and offer free drinks.

Thanks as well for giving me the opportunity to explore the local laundromat in our neighborhood, which became necessary as I was sick for a week and my children had no clean clothes. If not for your actions I would not have met Fred, the wino who hangs out in front of the laundromat, which is, conveniently for him, next to the liquor store. Fred graciously offered to sort my delicates for me. I declined his generous offer, so he moved on to another patron of the laundromat, who declined his request for spare change. Fred left abruptly, but not before making a few parting comments. While I do relish meeting my neighbors, I'm less fond of being accosted and told I have a sweet ass. But then again, what's a neighborhood without its colorful characters?

Speaking of which, I also got to meet a local police officer. I must confess I had never met one, so this was a thrill, despite the fact that the circumstances centered around a struggle with what I can only assume was someone in need who tried to take my clean clothes out of the dryer while I was outside on the phone. Apparently, according to Officer Grimes, taking someone else's property is frowned upon. This was an educational experience as well, as I learned something about the law. I even got to solidify my relationship with Officer Grimes, who showed up at my door after I reported that someone had broken into my apartment while I was at the laundromat. How fortunate for me that I had little of value except for my computer and printer, which, being stolen necessitated this note being handwritten. When I asked Officer Grimes about the possibility of getting my property back, he stifled a laugh.

Heading back downstairs to get my mail I saw that there was still a line of people waiting to use the washers. How fortunate that you were going to have the opportunity to get to know the people with whom you live. You must have hit it off well because it seemed like they were clearly planning something, possibly a party for you. I assumed they were discussing the menu when I heard one of our neighbors say, "It'll serve her right."

Remember Me, Or Don't

While I still have a week or so before I'm completely incoherent, I thought I would give you a heads up on my memorial service. By now you all know that I won't be around much longer. To save everyone the hassle of a wake and funeral, there will be a simple memorial service in the college chapel. In all honesty, I wouldn't have even had that, but my sister Dale insisted.

It's scheduled for the second Wednesday in May. I don't want this to drag into Memorial Day or to screw up everyone's weekend plans. In case you're making dinner plans for that day, don't worry. The service will be starting at 6:30 and you should be out in an hour. And if you're already committed to something else during that time, no worries. You do you.

If you're considering coming in from out of town-don't. You don't need to be spending the money. It's not like there will be a bunch of people standing around telling funny or heartwarming stories about me. If they do, I'm sure they'll be done in ten minutes. On the other hand, if you want to use the service as an excuse to get together with old pals from the neighborhood, then be my guest. Glad I could help.

If you really feel you need to be there, please don't feel you have to get up and say something. If you're getting this, I'm sure we had a good relationship, but let's face it, it's not like I snatched you out of the jaws of a crocodile. If you feel you must, then say what you will, but please don't embellish. Everyone will know it's bullshit. The truth is, I didn't accomplish much, I was an okay friend, and the day after I die the earth will still be spinning and you'll continue to put off your colonoscopy.

Oh, and if you're thinking of coming to see me before I'm dead, please don't. None of you have been in touch with me for over a year. In fairness, I haven't reached out to any of you either, so let's just call it a wash. Besides, I guarantee it won't make either of us feel better.

This all goes for my family as well. Please don't get on a plane for this. We've pretty much ignored each other for the past five years, ever since the last kid got married and I made my obligatory appearance.

The only exception I would make is that if you want to come and help my sister out, I'd appreciate it. She's the only family I have in the area so she feels obligated to do what she thinks is "the right thing."

I'm too weak to fight with her, so, like…whatever.

So please accept this "get out of jail free" card as my parting gift to you.

You're off the hook.

Of course, I'm sure none of you will appreciate this as it's unlikely you will have read it.

Remotely Interested

Gwen stands behind the couch, watching her husband Arthur flip

channels on the remote with alarming speed. She'd seen him do this

many times over their thirty years of marriage, but for some reason,

tonight she stands transfixed as the images on the screen fly by.

"I thought you were going to bed," Arthur says without looking up.

"I was, but I wanted to see what captivated you so much that you're not."

"I was watching something but then I lost interest."

"Given the flipping around you're doing it seems that there's not much you're interested in."

"Well, I find something that looks interesting, I watch for a few minutes, and then I get bored."

"So instead of giving it some time to see if it might hold your interest, you just abandon it and move on to something else?"

"Well, that's the beauty of cable," says Arthur. "There's so much to choose from."

"Maybe so but it seems like you're spending an awful lot of energy to try to give yourself a small amount of satisfaction."

Gwen sits down next to her husband. Arthur doesn't react. His gaze at the television is unwavering.

"Looking for something new and different is better than watching all those reruns of *Law and Order,*" he says. "You know how every episode will play out. You can practically recite the dialogue verbatim."

"Yes," Gwen replies, "but there's something very satisfying about that. I'm never disappointed. When I watch, I can relax and really enjoy it."

"But don't you miss the excitement of discovering something new?"

"No. Most of your searching leads to disappointment. Why expend all that energy on what's most likely to be a waste of time?"

"Because that one thing you find will be more exciting and fulfilling than the sameness of those old reruns."

"You do all this searching and to what end? So you can watch by yourself? If you want to watch with me, I've got to find the show interesting too."

"If I have to, I can watch by myself."

"Are you saying that you'd rather enjoy what you're doing by yourself?"

Silence.

Finally, Arthur looks at her. "Well, there's some satisfaction there, but it's not the same thing. It's better with you"

"I'm glad to hear you say that."

"It's just that you don't seem interested in exploring other possibilities."

"I would, but most of the things you gravitate to don't interest me."

"How do you know until you've tried?" Arthur asks.

"Maybe I would if you weren't so quick with the remote."

"I generally go faster when I'm by myself."

Gwen responds, "Well, I'm trying to tell you that going faster doesn't work for me."

"You can't expect me to watch with you if you're only tuning in to the same shows over and over again," Arthur counters.

"You used to watch with me all the time."

"Yes, but after so many years, I need a little change of pace."

"Have your needs changed that much?" Gwen asks.

"You know I love watching reruns with you-but it would be nice if you'd at least entertain the idea of watching something new with me."

"Most of the new things you gravitate to, make me uncomfortable."

"You used to have more of an adventurous spirit."

"Maybe my tastes have changed," Gwen answers. "It seems like a waste of time looking for new things when I know what's going to make me happy."

"What about what's going to make *me* happy?" Arthur asks.

"I thought you'd be happy if I were happy."

"I am. But why doesn't that work both ways? Shouldn't we both be trying to make each other happy?"

"You know what? That's a good point." Gwen says. "We should."

"So, what does that mean?" Arthur says, putting down the remote and looking at her.

"I guess." Gwen answers, "it means that one person can't necessarily meet all the needs of their partner, no matter how much the two of them love each other,"

"That's certainly sobering."

"Well, Arthur, that's real life and maybe we should just face it."

"So, what are we going to do?"

Gwen looks at Arthur for a moment, stands, and holds out her hand. "First, I think we should go into the bedroom and make love. And I'll put on the nurse outfit you got me from Victoria's Secret."

"I thought you told me you were uncomfortable wearing it."

"In the spirit of compromise and adventure I'm willing to give it a try."

Arthur's face lights up. "Great."

"But next time, it's no costumes and the lights are out. And you'd better not phone it in. Deal?"

"Deal," Arthur replies. "I love you."

"I love you too." Gwen leads Arthur towards the bedroom but then stops.

"Oh, and when we're done, we're going to order another television."

The Existential Angst of a Toyota Corolla

It's been a month and I have barely moved. Why did he retire? I thought I'd enjoy being parked in the building garage. It's warm, safe, and dry. But it's so boring. The motorcycle parked next to me thinks she's so cool. Well, I guess she is. She's out almost every day and comes back with a windblown look.

***

Oh, the places we used to go!: The Berkshires for the changing leaves; Montauk for the long stretches of beach; the Pocono Mountains. They all are a distant memory.

***

I feel like I'm wasting away. If he doesn't drive me soon, I'll never get going. Is it asking too much for him to at least come down here and warm me up? I can feel my fuel pump atrophying. Does gas evaporate?

***

The Hyundai thinks he's hot stuff because he drove to Boca Raton. Big deal. What did you see, twenty miles of pickleball courts?

***

The other cars are shunning me. The Ford Explorer said I was a "waste of a parking space." The Honda and I were so close. Now she's not even speaking to me. I am in despair.

***

I've got layers of dirt and grime building up. I need to get cleaned. Someone wrote "wash me" in the dust on my windshield. It's humiliating.

***

Finally, I can see the light of day. I don't even care about the potholes on Pelham Road. But we've only gone as far as the supermarket. I need to get on the highway.

***

At last, the car wash. I guess taking me out, he saw how dirty I was. I feel like a new car.

***

I've never been so glad to see the New England Thruway. At noon, there's no rush hour traffic so we're just zipping north into Connecticut. We've just passed two Range Rovers and a tractor-trailer. I feel so alive!

***

What's that noise?

***

That sticker on the windshield is not for decoration. Change my damn oil! I feel like I'm getting creakier by the minute.

***

Back in the garage. He is walking away from me. When will I see the light of day again? I hear my doors lock as he clicks the remote control. My future is a terrifying mystery.

The Holiday Solution

For the past I don't know how many years, I've shown up at my sister's home for Thanksgiving, where her nuclear family prepare the annual gorge-fest attended by my mom, my aunt, my brother and his brood, and whatever stray person my sister has befriended throughout the year. Occasionally they would invite a single woman to see if anything would develop between the guest and me. No sparks ever ignited, and eventually the project to pair me up came to a merciful end.

My family doesn't see very much of me throughout the year, so on this day they're obligated to ask about my life. I never have anything interesting to report. I've been at the same dead-end job and same apartment for many years. My declaration, last Thanksgiving, that I've watched every episode of *Law & Order* did not seem to generate any conversation.

By the time everyone has had a few glasses of wine the drilling down into my life starts. "Are you still at that job?" "What do you do with your time?" "You still in that same apartment?" and of course, "So when are you getting married?" I suffer through this each year out of a sense of obligation. My mom will occasionally try to stem the onslaught of questions with the statement, "He just hasn't found his purpose yet." I know I'm not the only one who goes through this because I hear some of the same stories from the guys at Chumley's Bar.

This year, however, I came up with a solution. And it was just pure luck. About six months ago, one of the guys from the bar brought his cousin Frank with him to hang out one Sunday to watch the game. Frank turned out to be a very interesting guy. The reason I know this is because Frank will tell you his life story at the drop of a hat. It's actually quite a story. Frank came from the same neighborhood but grew up in foster care, aged out, and just drifted. He was in a gang for a while and had numerous (non-violent) brushes with the law, and eventually went to jail for stealing a car. While in jail he started college and turned his life around. He finished college while working as a limo driver and eventually bought the company. He now arranges rides for the rich and famous.

As I sat in the bar that Sunday, I decided to ask Frank if he wanted to come to Thanksgiving at my sister's. He's got no family to speak of and I have more than I need. My sister was more than happy for me to bring Frank along. She had no strays to include this year and seemed to be glad I was at least having some human interaction outside of work.

Frank wasted no time ingratiating himself to my family. He brought excellent wine, and pastries from one of the better bakeries downtown. With only the smallest opening in the pre-dinner conversation, Frank managed to introduce the tragic circumstances of his birth and time spent in foster care. As we sat down to eat the family heard about his nefarious exploits as a teenager, and his time spent incarcerated. My family listened to all of this with their mouths agape. How could this well-spoken well-dressed man have done all of these things? Just when my sister was afraid she was harboring a criminal, Frank launched into his redemption story. By the time dessert came he was regaling those around the table with his brushes with the likes of Lebron, Leo, and Taylor.

By this time, the focus was so far off of me that I was able to escape to my niece's bedroom, open the window, and smoke enough weed to get me through what remained of the day. I had entertained nary a question or comment about my meaningless life. By the time we said good night my brother-in-law was desperately trying to extract a promise from Frank that he would be back. This was the best Thanksgiving I've had in years.

The next day it occurred to me that I'm probably not the only one suffering through an agonizing family holiday. Could I be of service to more people like me? I can't clone Frank, but maybe I can find more people like him who have overcome all the odds against them and come out on top. Once I find those folks, I simply put out an ad:

Holidays Got You Down?

Are you a disappointment to your family? Need to take the attention away from yourself during the holidays? Bring the self-made person to your next holiday celebration. They will regale your friends and family with tales of their hardscrabble upbringing; their arduous ascent to the top rung of their industry; and their self-satisfied success. They will share their harrowing experiences as well as brushes with the rich and famous. Guaranteed to take the focus so far off of you that everyone will forget you're even present. This will allow you to go outside and ingest enough gummies to tolerate the festivities. Choose from all genders, races, religions, ethnic groups, and political persuasions.

Hey, maybe I do have a purpose in life.

The Reluctant Party Animal

Okay, that's it. I'm going to the party.

I want to see my friends! So of course, I have to go. But this is the first time I'll be in the same room as Amy since the breakup. It's been a year, but I still don't know if I'm ready for this and she'll probably bring her new boyfriend. Won't that be fun!

I can take some comfort in the likelihood that everyone will probably sympathize with me. After all, she did dump me. But do I want to put myself through this?

No, but I've got to go. My absence would be too conspicuous. I can just imagine what people would say. "Poor guy. He just can't bear seeing Amy with anyone else." Or, "he's probably taking a break from socializing until he heals." "Yeah, we don't see Barry anymore. He just sits in his sweatpants, eating Cherry Garcia and watching Bassmasters on ESPN."

Screw that, I'm going.

So, what if I do see Amy? Let's review my options: Door number one: I could ignore her. Of course, this will mean I'll have to figure out where she is at all times which seems like a lot of work. Door number two: I could go right up to her and say hello, introduce myself to the guy she left me for, utter a few pleasantries, and walk away. This will leave her boyfriend to ask, "who was that?" and she'll have to explain it. Given the fact that I hear they're having problems, that should cause some tension.

Nah, that's a little mean. Door number three: I can just go to the party, touch base with my friends, catch up, have a few drinks and some food and if I happen to bump into Amy, I just play it by ear. Who am I kidding? It's gotta be number three.

Okay. I made it to the party. Here I am!

I am not going to look for her. I am not going to look for her. I am not going to look for her. Of course, if she's at the party I'll probably hear her voice. But I don't *want* to hear it. Okay, I need to talk to someone, anyone, so I can focus on something other than Amy. There's Peter. Great. He'll talk about his wife, Gloria, who left him three years ago after 17 years of marriage, for an accountant, and they moved to Vancouver, and that's all he'll talk about. There is no other subject. It doesn't matter what you bring up, he'll find a way to make it about Gloria.

"Hey, Peter, how's it going?"

"I'm kind of blue. You know, next week, would have been our 20th anniversary"

"That's a tough one."

"I had a special vacation planned."

"Really?"

"Yeah…I guess that's not going to happen."

"No, I suppose not."

I don't want to be mean. But I got to get him to talk about something else. Something that has nothing to do with Gloria.

"Hey, the Jets game tomorrow should be really good," I say.

"You know Gloria, had a Jets jersey. She wore it every Sunday. She looked so cute in it."

I'm in hell. How did he do that?

"I still have it in our closet."

I hope this isn't me, three years from now.

"You know what? I'm going to get another drink."

And here's Janet. Married, uber-successful. Husband's been a struggling actor for twenty-five years. Go to give him credit for hanging in.

"Hey Barry, how are you doing?"

She obviously feels sorry for me. How can I tell? It's the tone of her question, the hand on my arm, what she's actually asking is, "How are you doing you poor baby, and how did you manage, to climb out of the wreckage of your life and make your way to this party?"

"Doing great" I proceed to make my work promotion sound like I won a MacArthur genius grant.

"That's terrific," Janet replies, not having the vaguest idea of what I'm talking about.

"Yeah, and I'm going to Mexico in February."

"That's great"

I'm doing no such thing, but that should get around the party quickly.

Here's an idea for a drinking game: Every time I need to extricate myself from a conversation I don't want to be having, I take a drink. I should be passed out in about an hour.

Now I'm in the kitchen and everyone is laughing. Larry is telling one of his stories about how dumb his boss is. They all must have started drinking much earlier cause he's not that funny.

All in all, I'm glad I showed up. I'm at least giving the impression that I'm fine and that I could care less whether Amy's here or not.

Then, as if by magic, Amy appears right in front of me.

"Hi, how's it going?"

I take a big gulp of my drink.

"Fine. Can we talk for a minute?"

I nod and Amy walks toward the garden.

Is this where she says she made a big mistake and wants to get back together?

"I feel like there's something I need to tell you," she says.

I say nothing because I don't want her to stop talking.

"I learned a lot this year. One of the things I learned is that relationships take a lot of work. And that was work I wasn't prepared to do with you. I know we've both moved on…

We have?

…but I wanted to let you know that I can acknowledge my part in our breakup and I'm working to not let that happen again. Maybe if I was willing to do the work before we wouldn't have broken up. I just need you to know whatever happened wasn't just you.

I'm crushed and gratified at the same time. I can't be mad. It's time to take the high road.

"Thanks for telling me that. I really appreciate it.

And I mean it.

"I hope things work out for you and Fred."

I almost mean that, but I'll work on it.

TMI from my GPS

Barely speaking to each other, my wife and I headed out to make an appearance at the christening of my niece's son. The silence was a combination of my defensiveness and my wife's passive-aggressive behavior, stemming from my not having my cell phone on. To say that neither of us was looking forward to this event was an understatement.

I am very bad at directions, so I always put my faith in my GPS. So much faith that I just sprang for a deluxe model with enhanced features. I got a model with ear pods in so that my wife could listen to music. I am so fond of my GPS that I named it Radar, a character in the movie and television show M*A*S*H*. Radar always knew what was coming before everyone else.

No sooner had I started the car than I heard the following from Radar:

You're going to be so late. Start thinking up excuses for your niece other than the truth, which is you wouldn't leave until you finished watching the end of the Eagles game.

At the post-christening party we stayed on opposite sides of the room to avoid the temptation to bicker, and managed to leave as soon as we could, but not so early as to generate family gossip. I thought about suggesting we go to the movies, but as soon as we got in the car, I heard Radar in my earpiece:

You're both in a foul mood and going to the movies will not make it any better. You will not enjoy yourselves. Just cut your losses and go home.

As I started driving, Radar was in my ear again.

You should probably apologize or it's going to be a very long day.

Fearing that this silence would go on for an indeterminant period, I decided to offer an olive branch. But my own stubbornness would only let me issue a "non-apology:" an offer to drive out to the beach, which I know my wife loves but I only tolerate. A fact she knows well. I hoped that looking out at the ocean together for a few hours would somehow get us back to a place that would allow us to communicate beyond "pass the salt." No sooner were we on our way when I heard from Radar again:

Your trip to the beach is a waste of time. When you get there, it will start raining and not stop until tomorrow morning. Just go home.

Determined to prove him wrong, I continued on. A mile or so further, flashing lights indicated that traffic would soon come to a stop. While I decided what to do, Radar strongly offered his advice.

Don't even think about getting off the highway. Trust me. This way will be faster.

Of course, in my stubbornness, I ignored him and got off the highway.

Okay, be that way. Now you'll be sitting in traffic for another hour.

With my wife still silent, and traffic not moving, I looked around for something to distract me until I heard from Radar again.

Keep your eyes on the road. Stop eyeing the redhead in the Jaguar. You're in enough trouble as it is. Plus, you'll notice her husband is built like a refrigerator with feet.

Then, of course, it started raining.

I told you last week to get new wipers. But did you listen? No.

Obviously, this was turning out not to be a beach day, so we agreed to head home. Now the traffic going in the other direction, toward home, had slowed down.

Pull Into the next rest stop. If you think you're going to make it home without a bathroom break, you're sorely mistaken.

This time I listened. Once we were back on the road. Radar had more advice to give.

Now that you've screwed up the day, the least you can do is cook dinner tonight. Turn left to go to the supermarket. Don't make the next right. Some idiot decided to park in the middle of a two-lane road. If you hit the car, the insurance company will blame you.

We reached the supermarket and, taking credit for Radar's suggestion, told my wife to wait in the car and listen to music while I shopped. Returning with the necessary supplies for the dinner I would make, I could sense my wife softening in response to my effort. Maybe we could salvage the day. So, we headed home, in a better mood than when we left.

When Radar started talking to me, I abruptly turned him off, and in my head, I said, "Thanks, I can take it from here."

Woman Rejects Sister as Bridesmaid
as She Doesn't Have 'The Look'

I want to thank all the people on Reddit who have come to my defense. So many of you called my sister a b**ch that I don't have to. Sure, I was hurt not to be included in a wedding party that has ten bridesmaids, but I thought, okay, she's got friends she certainly spends more time with than me. (Although I felt that the woman from the nail salon who she knows for six months was a reach).

When I told my sister that it would be a nice gesture to include me as one of the bridesmaids (I probably should be the maid of honor seeing how her current one seems completely uninterested, but, whatever), she said I would throw off the "look" she wants to create because of my size. (I'm a 10 for crying out loud, not that it should matter.) Yes, I'm bigger than the perpetually starving stick figures who are her "friends," but c'mon!

My sister actually sent out an email to the bridesmaids insisting on specific hair length and color, nail length and color, and their dress size not to exceed a 4. She further advised them that if they had put on any weight they should get to the gym as she had already picked out their dresses.

No, we've never been super close. She was always the thin, popular girl, and I was the plain nerd. She spent the years we went to the same school staying as far away from me as possible, just short of denying that we were related. But it still hurts. And just as I'm getting to a place where I can make peace with this, my sister, in a panic, comes to me to ask me to plan the wedding. Apparently, her maid of honor and bridesmaids have completely dropped the ball around the planning they were supposed to do for the bachelorette party and the wedding. She was counting on them to take care of all the details. But no one had the time. Yes, I'm an event planner, but when she was putting together her wedding, she had no interest in my input. Now she's come to me and asked me to take over the whole thing. When I asked if this means she was including me in the bridal party she said, yes, as long as I grew my nails, cut my hair, and lost thirty pounds by October. Not gonna happen. Yes, I'm hurt. So if she wants to treat me like a hired hand, then I decided to act like one and told her that I would do it only if she would pay me a fee to be her wedding planner. She went crazy and cried to our parents. Our family has called me selfish and accused me of ruining my sister's wedding. She put this on social media and, while there are people sticking up for me, there are also people telling me what a horrible person I am.

I don't know why.

I gave her a very reasonable rate.

You Know I Can Hear You, Right?

Lou used to be a friendly, outgoing guy. He loved his work as the manager of an appliance store. But then a toaster oven fell on his head. He was knocked unconscious for a short while. When he came to, he seemed fine; achy, but otherwise unhurt. However, he did notice one stark change.

The first time he noticed the change was when he went to a local butcher shop. When he walked in the door he thought "Something's gone bad in here." At which the butcher ran up to Lou, and wagged his finger in Lou's face, saying "don't start trouble. There's nothing wrong in here."

Lou was stunned, but soon he realized that, after a few similar incidents, because of the accident, he now had trouble knowing whether he was speaking out loud, or just thinking to himself. Dealing with people created nothing but problems for him and anyone with whom he came into contact. Even simple interactions like going through the checkout line in the grocery store led to people angrily confronting him about his "unuttered" thoughts. Lou decided that the only way to get through life without conflict was to avoid personal interactions at all costs.

The worst part of his new affliction was that he could no longer attend the Broadway theatres he loved so much. He would usually go to two or three plays in a month. Now he was terrified about what might happen if he tried to take in a show. He stayed away from the theatre for months, but when a new play opened to unanimous raves, Lou could no longer resist. He ordered his tickets by mail and hoped he'd be able to attend the show without causing harm to others or himself.

When Lou arrived at the theatre, he took his seat in the balcony and hoped there would be no one sitting next to him. He looked at his watch repeatedly, willing the time to move faster so the show would start, and the seats next to him would be empty. With two minutes to go, Lou thought he was home free when an older couple approached his row.

"Excuse me," the man said. Lou stood to make room for the couple to get to their seats. He was careful not to make eye contact. but he couldn't help but notice the woman's handbag. It was a poorly made Gucci knockoff. She probably bought it from a peddler in Times Square.

"Another sucker," he thought.

The woman turned to Lou and demanded sharply,

"What did you say?"

"Who, me? I was just saying you're rather lucky to get a ticket," Lou replied.

The lights went down, and the play began. It was a comedy about local politics. Lou felt that the first act was great but that the performance of the lead actress was terrible. "How did she ever get cast?" Lou thought, "she's terrible. Is she the producer's niece? The understudy is probably better." No sooner had this thought crossed his mind than the man seated in front of him turned around and glared at him, "would you mind keeping your opinions to yourself? I'm trying to enjoy the play. If you want to make nasty comments, stay home and watch television."

Cringing with humiliation, Lou escaped from his seat to the lobby. While he was deciding whether he would go back into the theatre for the second act, the first act ended, and the audience spilled out into the lobby. A couple in their 30s passed by him. The man was tall and athletic, the woman, a stunning, brunette. She was so beautiful that Lou couldn't help but let his mind wander, and think, "Wow, "you have an incredible body.

Suddenly there was blackness. As he opened his eyes, Lou felt a deep, dull pain in his jaw. The next thing he knew he was on the floor, looking up at the man, fist clenched who was saying, "Talk to my wife like that again and I'll hit you so hard…you won't be able to walk."

Lou staggered out of the theatre, discouraged by what a disappointing and painful evening this had turned out to be. He made his way back to the subway. The minute he sat down in the train car, Lou took his phone out, determined not to look at anyone or anything. Unfortunately, his phone had no signal. Lou panicked. He tried to find something innocuous to focus on, but his eyes were drawn to his fellow passengers.

There was a young woman sitting across from him with turquoise hair and multiple piercings. "Why on earth would anyone do that to themselves?" Lou thought before he could stop himself. He braced for her angry response. The woman looked up at him, sighed, and rolled her eyes. But then, a moment later he noticed a businessman-type sporting an obvious comb-over. "Shave your head. Lou thought. You look ridiculous." The man glanced over at Lou, shaking his head as if Lou was the one who should be pitied. Still nervous about a confrontation, Lou walked to the other end of the train car where he saw a twentysomething couple enthusiastically making out. "Oh, get a room," Lou thought and stopped short as the couple unlocked from their embrace, looked at him, laughed, and reattached themselves to each other.

It occurred to Lou that he finally found the one place he could go and think about anything he wanted without anyone even blinking: The New York City Subway.

Lou smiled. He was home.

Your Turn

The Ft. Lauderdale Sun-Times devotes this space to our readers. We invite you to send in your thoughts about life in southeastern Florida. These columns are not censored but may be edited for clarity. Reader David Tarnower offers the following thoughts.

If you're a single middle-aged heterosexual male you've probably been inundated with news about "toxic masculinity," "the patriarchy," and other nonsense designed to emasculate us. Having been in the dating pool, successfully, for a number of years, and been through three marriages, I have some advice, and you'd be wise to listen up. Especially if you've been out of the dating scene for a while. I call this:

The Real Man's Guide to Dating

One caveat: Don't skim this! Read all the way through to the end.

Who is in the pool?

Everyone you meet will be divorced. If you meet someone over thirty-five who has never been married, she's probably suffering from some form of mental illness. If you don't want to get stabbed in your sleep, just stay away.

When you're dating a woman who's divorced, you need to find out if she dumped her ex or if he dumped her. If she got kicked to the curb, she'll take all that anger out on you. Especially if you're the first guy she's dated since the divorce. If you find yourself in that situation, extricate yourself until she's cycled through a few relationships. Then she may be ready to be a reasonable companion. If she dumped her husband, be careful. She may have been brainwashed by some pro-feminist nonsense.

History: Yes or No?

Some people feel that everyone should start a relationship with a blank slate. "The past is the past. No need to explore it." This is a bad idea.

You need to hear all about her past relationships. If she's had more than three sexual partners, she's promiscuous and will almost certainly cheat on you.

Talk about how attractive and successful your last girlfriend is. This will keep your new one on her toes and make her up her game.

Feel free to tell her how generous you are with your alimony. Even if you aren't, it will make you look good and will also put her on alert that you don't have unlimited funds to spend on her.

If she mentions her ex more than once, she's either still hung up on him or challenging you to live up to his standard. Either way, get out fast.

Kids—Yours

Your children (until they're independent) will always be your priority. But hold off on introducing them to your new gal pal, until she's hooked on you. That way she'll be less likely to be turned off by their depression, sullen behavior, and ADHD. You're entitled to have a life, so if they become too much of a pain, just forget to pick them up on some of your weekends. Let their mother straighten them out.. You didn't want them to begin with.

Kids—Hers

Put off meeting them for as long as possible. You can always stall this by claiming sensitivity to their accepting a new man into their mother's life.

Try to be "busy with work stuff" on weekends when she has her kids and free when she doesn't.

No matter how much you want to have sex, don't push to stay over when she's got the kids. If you do, it will create a sense of intimacy you don't want. The sex won't be good anyway.

Under no circumstances should you go on a family vacation with her kids (or with yours, for that matter).

The Truth

There seems to be little to say about this, as we all know it's always best to be truthful. However, there are many occasions where being truthful or honest is nothing but cruel.

This does not apply if your new partner should put on a few pounds. Tell her immediately. After all, you're concerned for her health. If she doesn't get rid of the pounds, get rid of her.

If she asks if the hostess seating you at a restaurant is attractive, don't hold back. She needs to know what you find appealing.

There are times when a little lie is fine. If she asks, "Does this make me look fat?" Just lie. The truth will just bring tears and you won't have sex for at least two weeks. (But you'll have dumped her by that time anyway).

Friends—Yours

If your friends liked your ex, and especially if you ended the relationship for reasons they don't quite get, you might have to ease someone new into the mix. This also means you didn't do a good job of trashing her when you broke up.

If your friends did not like the person you were seeing (including your wife), anything goes. Anyone you introduce them to will be welcomed with open arms. Except for your single guy friends who will be pissed if you're not hanging around with them as much. But you can reassure them that after the courting period, you'll be back to spending most evenings at the pub.

Friends—Hers

For many women, introducing a new guy to their friends has the same importance, if not more, as introducing him to her parents. At this point in her life, her friend's opinions matter even more. Therefore, there is an important strategy to deal with her friends that will make their presence in her life totally irrelevant in terms of your relationship. Your approach should be to exhibit as much (fake) enthusiasm for her friends as you can stomach, asking about their lives, and giving the impression of concern for them. Basically, everything short of flirting. They will not trash you, but give you the benefit of doubt in any concern your girlfriend expresses. In short order you will be a non-topic of discussion in their circle, which translates to less drama for you.

Gifts

Gifts are one of the social conventions most couples tacitly agree to participate in. Gifts come slathered in meaning…to the woman. There are only two no-nos: appliances and lingerie. Both will be thrown back in your face in a New York minute. Outside of those, it doesn't matter what the gift is as long as it's extremely expensive. If she likes it, she can flaunt it to her friends. If it's not her taste, it still tells her she's worth a lot and you'll be forgiven, because…well, you're a guy.

Sex

This isn't about will she or won't she. It's about when. Try to circle the bases as soon as possible. You don't want to waste a lot of time and money if she's a dud in the sack. If that's the case, get out as soon as you can. You don't want to be doing remedial sex instruction. On the other hand, if she's freaky, enjoy it for a while, but be ready to bolt. You know the old saying, "Crazy in bed…crazy in the head."

Social Media

It goes without saying: close all your social media accounts. The last thing you need is for your new gal to see the post made by that pharmaceutical sales rep in Phoenix.

One last thing: Now that you've absorbed these important teachings, you're ready to go out into the world of middle-aged dating. Remember these lessons <u>and do exactly the opposite of everything you've read here.</u>

You're Not Welcome

Phrase Eliminated from English Language

"You're Welcome" has officially been replaced
with "No Problem"

Lack of shock expressed by linguists, educators, and writers

A confidential source has leaked the information that in an unprecedented decision Merriam-Webster Dictionary announced that its 11th edition will no longer include the phrase "You're Welcome." Despite the fact that for over a century, people in the English-speaking world have been using this expression to respond to one person expressing thanks to another, Merriam-Webster's has determined that the phrase is antiquated, and so rarely uttered as to render current speakers of this phrase likely to be foreign spies or extraterrestrials.

For decades, "you're welcome" had become so deeply ingrained as to be reflexive. Recipients of a "thank you" would respond with the expression without thinking. Research has shown that when questioned, only seven percent of people surveyed were even aware that they uttered this phrase. However, in recent years, the phrase has all but disappeared from the lexicon.

According to the Oxford English Dictionary, the first citation of "you're welcome" is seen in 1907. However, there are references dating back to the fourteenth century, deriving from the Old English *wilcuma*, a noun meaning "a desired guest." It is believed that the term originated with customers patronizing London's first brothel.

Replacing this antiquated form of acknowledging thanks, the dictionary will now include the term "no problem," adjudged to be in wide use throughout the fifty states as well as in American Samoa. With the expansion of the service economy worldwide, companies want their representatives to supply good customer service. In the language of the twenty-first century, a restaurant patron saying "thank you" after a server takes their order will invariably get the response "no problem," rather than "your welcome." Similarly, someone saying "thank you" after successfully ordering merchandise over the phone, or making an appointment with a doctor's office, will most likely hear "no problem."

This expression is now so ingrained in the current lexicon that the "script" given to customer service representatives includes acknowledging requests for service by saying "no problem" after every response.

Academics are asserting that this shift confirms Wittgenstein's **idea** that our particular assignment of meaning comes from the cultural and social constructs surrounding us.

"This change reflects the resentment of those in service positions who bitterly resent doing the job they're paid for," said President and CEO of Merriam's, William Wordsmith, "this change is long overdue. I haven't heard anyone say 'you're welcome' in fifteen years. Then again, I haven't thanked anyone for anything in twenty years."

While this development has gone largely unnoticed, the makers of WELCOME mats have been barraging Merriam-Webster's offices with calls and letters and have gone so far as to put up a billboard, one block from the company's headquarters in Springfield, Massachusetts. It reads, "Oh yes, there's a problem."

Section Three: THINGS I THINK I THINK

11 Things I'll Never Do

At 75, it would be very easy to point to activities like bungee jumping, and say, "I'm too old to do that." But I cannot, in good conscience, blame the calendar on my reluctance to create a bucket list of once-in-a-lifetime thrills. As much as I would like to excuse myself from this exercise by producing my birth certificate, the plain truth is that I'm not taking on any of the life-affirming challenges that my contemporaries are embracing because I DON'T WANT TO DO ANY OF THOSE THINGS, AND IN FACT NEVER DID.

In order to save the time of friends and family members who would like to recruit me to accompany them on their new and wonderous adventures, I have compiled an Anti-Bucket List—a list of stuff I'm just not going to do, so don't bother to ask.

1. **Sky Diving**. I feel about sky diving the way former Ohio State football coach Woody Hayes felt about the forward pass. "Only three things can happen and two of them are bad." If you can manage to step out of a plane and into thin air, you will, either 1) survive; 2) fall and break both your legs; or 3) crash to the earth and die. Not being an optimist, I think I'll stay in my seat. In the best of circumstances, sky diving reminds me of when I lost my virginity: Anxiety, insecurity, and a few minutes of fun. I have no desire to relive that.

2. **Bungee Jumping**. see Sky Diving

3. **Traveling to the Holy Land**. People of all faiths have described this to me as a supremely spiritual experience. I'll take their word for it. Personally, I prefer not getting blown to bits while I'm having a slice of pizza.

4. **Learning a foreign language**. At first, this actually sounded like a good idea. I envisioned myself traveling to a foreign country, being able to get directions from the locals and not winding up at a plumbing supply store, ordering off a menu, and not being told that I just asked for a side of tractors. Then I realized that even if I could learn to speak another language, with my hearing loss, I wouldn't be able to hear anyone speaking to me. (Frankly, I can barely understand anyone speaking English to me anymore).

5. **Sailing around the world**. Bad idea. I get seasick. I've tried patches, pills, and injections, all to no avail. If I want to spend that much time inside a bathroom, I'll have a colonoscopy.

6. **Moving to a foreign country**. "The cost of living is so much cheaper" is the refrain I always hear. The way I look at it, all the money I'll save in a third-world country probably won't be enough to pay the ransom when I'm kidnapped. Yes, medical

care is cheaper too, but I barely trust the doctors here. What am I going to do when I can't even explain what my symptoms are? And do you have any idea how long it took me to find a good dentist?

7. **Running a marathon**. Oh, please. Jim Fixx started the running craze in this country and died of a heart attack at 52. While he was running. I already have heart issues and I'm 75. Anyway, I perform the equivalent of a marathon every two weeks if you add up the miles I put on going to the bathroom each night. So that's a hard pass.

8. **Buying a motorcycle and driving wherever the road leads till I make my way across the country**. No part of that sentence interests me. I'd rather watch *Easy Rider*. And if I want to get lost, I'll go to Home Depot.

9. **Reading the great books**. Really?? Slog through twelve hundred pages of Tolstoy? I'll be dead before I find out what happens in the end. Instead, I can watch it on Netflix and be done before lunch.

10. **Volunteering.** Hey, I don't see people lining up to help *me*. Instead, maybe somebody can read the great books to me and watch me fall asleep.

11. **Spending more time with my kids.** Screw 'em. They all moved as far away from me as they could possibly get.

I can't imagine why.

Stay in Your Lane, AAA

I recently read an article in AAA magazine called *55 Reasons It's Great to Be Over 55.*

Is that so.

According to the writers, these 55 things are automatically conferred on you when you hit this magic age. I beg to differ. Here's just a sampling of their pronouncements.

"People trust your opinion."

Yeah, not so much. Many people will discount your opinion *because* you're over 55. But it gets worse and not only that, a lot of people will use your age as a reason to do so. Especially if they don't agree with you. The Millennials in my office were recently arguing about great movies. When I said, *"Citizen Kane"* (the greatest movie ever made) they looked at me as if I were speaking Finnish.

"You welcome the heat."

I don't care how much sweat gland activity decreases as we age, if you weren't a fan of Florida's sweltering weather before you turned 55, you won't turn into one now. And unless you enjoy living in a sauna, Arizona is no better. I visited my in-laws one September in Phoenix. It was lovely in their air-conditioned house, but thirty seconds after I went outside, I wilted like month-old cabbage.

"You resolve conflicts skillfully."

There's no magic age at which you become a skilled diplomat. If you were good at conflict resolution before, there's no reason to think you won't continue to be. On the other hand, if you're bad at it, you won't turn into Nelson Mandela on your 55th birthday. My former boss, at 62, when faced with intraoffice difficulties, would go into his office and shut the door. Leaving the rest of us to re-enact *Lord of the Flies*. Big fun.

"Free time increases."

Free time increases only if you don't need to work — a circumstance that has become increasingly rare unless you're part of the 1% in which case you have nothing but free time and don't give a shit about any of this. For the rest of us, free time is figuring out how to avoid spending the rest of our days asking, "Do you want fries with that?"

"An empty nest means more time with your partner."

True. Unless your adult child has moved back in with you (another trending phenomenon). In which case you and your partner are going to spend all of that lovely "free time" trying to get them back out of the house. My friend Judy was just telling me how happy she was now that her 35-year-old son has moved back home. At least I think that's what she was trying to tell me. It was hard to make out what she was saying through her gritted teeth.

"Your close friendships are even closer."

Sure. Unless your close friends have died. Or have moved to Boca Raton. In which case, there's always Facebook. But let's face it, if they were really good friends, they wouldn't have moved away from you, so screw 'em. Luckily, this isn't an issue for me as I have no friends.

After reading this article, here's my take:

55 is way too young to be checking off the "older adult" box. Everyone I know who is 55 is still working. It's time to re-think what "older" is. Liam Neeson is 70 and he's spent his last three movies kicking asses on three continents.

There is plenty of advice online about when to retire and what to do, but I haven't read it.

I'm too busy working.

Career Path

There is universal acknowledgement that the career of a professional athlete is brief. Their earning potential can be reduced to zero with one injury. Unless one is playing at the highest level, many athletes need to supplement their income with other endeavors.

For the men and women of professional wrestling, there seems to be career path for which they are ideally suited, one that utilizes their gifts, experience, and resilience: Pornographic films. Before someone body slams me into the turnbuckle, I'm not saying that pro wrestling is pornographic. I am saying that the process of staging these activities, as well as the participants themselves, have much in common. So much so, that the qualities for success in pro wrestling are transferable to success in pornographic films.

For instance:

1. Ability of participants to feign pain and/or pleasure:

Before they get into the ring, wrestlers enroll in the Actor's Studio. As is strikingly obvious, many flunk out. Some, after numerous concussions, will star in dinner theatre productions of *Of Mice and Men* or *Gypsy*. Women in porn convincingly (?) demonstrate ecstasy while having their bodies pounded like a ten-penny nail into a two by four. Men in porn pretend to enjoy being whipped by women dressed in leather and speaking in a bad German accent.

2. Glistening, well-endowed men and women:

It would be no surprise to discover that various pro wrestling organizations have at least partial ownership in companies that produce the baby oil spread out in copious amounts over these endomorphic physiques. No doubt the men and many of the women are workout warriors, but steroids enhance their physiques to cartoon proportions. In porn, saline, and other enhancements create the equivalent of floatation devices on many women, in addition to the porn producers casting men and women who are genetic outliers in the area of secondary sexual characteristics.

3. Well-worn tropes

"I'm a storyteller," said every person putting something "dramatic" in front of an audience. In both porn and wrestling these stories are left over from cave paintings. In porn, it's the pizza delivery guy and the only topping is sausage. And of course, the plumber who is there to unclog pipes, and the pool boy to whom the woman of the house feels obliged to offer a cold drink. In pro wrestling it's the "Pretty Boy," "Aristocrat," "Anti-American Heel," "Loose Cannon," For women, some of the recurring characters include "Obsessive Psycho Chick," "Barbie," "Anti-Barbie," "Promiscuous Woman." Who you root for is up to you and your particular brand of kink.

4. Suspension of disbelief from the audience

Wrestling audiences have no trouble accepting the idea that a referee can have a prolonged conversation with one wrestler in the ring while a few feet away two wrestlers are ganging up on a third. I don't want to shortchange the referees who must, despite knowing what's taking place a few feet away from them and with thousands of people screaming at them to just turn around and look, pretend so effectively to be oblivious. Porn viewers routinely accept circumstances where two strangers agree within fifteen seconds of meeting to have sex, or that it's a common occurrence for women to enjoy sex acts with multiple partners. Why just the other day I walked into my office and an orgy was going on. Yeah, like that.

5. Extraordinary physical stamina

Despite the over-the-top histrionics, there is no denying that the men and women of pro wrestling are athletes in top condition who routinely absorb collisions with both other large people and inanimate objects. (These folks must get their health insurance from Lloyds of London). It's hard to imagine how porn stars can bring energy to their performances and manifest fake passion take after take. Eventually it must be like the equivalent of trying to breathe life into a CPR dummy.

6. **Willingness of participants to engage in risk-taking behavior.**

I don't care how much you work out, having 300-pound people fall on you will take its toll on your body. And there are only so many times you can fall on your head before you're not able to do anything except serve as a large doorstop. If you're on a porn set, a myriad of STDs wait to infect you, not to mention psycho stalkers who are convinced you're communicating with them through your videos.

There you have it. The next time a reporter asks a wrestler, "So what are you going to do now that you're hanging up your wrestling shoes?"

They can say, "I'm heading for the San Fernando Valley"- the porn capitol of the U.S.

Oh wait. One more thing pro wrestling has in common with porn movies:

7. No surprise endings

In pro wrestling the outcome is predetermined. It's a simple good guy/bad guy scenario. Like any action movie, the hero will be in some (fake) jeopardy but overcome it at the end. In hetero porn, the end is also a given. It comes when it comes.

IMHO

(In My Humble Opinion)

I'm a loyal reader of the Social Qs feature in the Sunday New York Times. I have nothing but admiration for Philip Galanes who responds to questions from people looking for advice on a variety of interpersonal dilemmas. I find Mr. Galanes's replies to be thoughtful and kind.

I must admit, however, that I find some of these questions he receives infuriating. These are the ones that contain, what I feel, are petty complaints- the thank you cards not received; the party snubs; the parents complaining that they can't control every aspect of the lives of their adult children and vice versa.

Sometimes I think, "Really, is that your biggest problem?" or "You mean you really can't figure out what the right thing is here?" But of course, Mr. Galanes would never write that. He handles these inquiries with patience and wisdom. I, on the other hand, would respond differently.

I'm raising my hand in case Mr. Galanes would like to take a vacation and have someone step in for him temporarily. Providing, of course, I'm able to have my own response to letters such as these which were actually sent to him. I already have a nom de plume, *The Listener.*

Dear Listener

I waited all my life for my son to bring home the girl he would marry and give me grandchildren. When he finally does, I can't abide her. Oh, she's polite, but she dresses inappropriately like she's still looking to attract a man. Worse, she refuses to eat my cooking. She just moves the food around on her plate and when I ask her if she likes it (of course I know the answer) she just says, "It's fine, I'm just not very hungry." Now that's just rude. I don't understand. She's educated, has a good job, and my son is apparently in love with her. I need to find a way to broach this with my son, so he can see the mistake he's making.

Concerned Mom

Dear Concerned Mom

No, you don't. Who made you the fashion police? If your son doesn't have an issue (and even if he does) it's none of your business. It's very likely, in fact, that he likes the way she dresses. He may encourage it. It might get their sexual engines churning. (Don't want to think about that do you?) As far as the food is concerned, maybe you're a lousy cook.

Dear Listener

Since I contacted Covid my taste buds have dulled. I went to dinner with friends where the cook made some lovely-looking dishes. I ate freely but couldn't taste anything, so I didn't say anything about the food. Should I tell her how disappointed I am in not being able to enjoy the cooking?

Numb Gums

Dear Numb Gums

Oh yeah sure. By all means. Make someone who knocked themselves out cooking feel bad. Oh, and make sure everyone else at the dinner hears you so that everyone can feel badly for you and make you the center of attention, ignoring the person who worked to prepare and cook a meal that everyone could enjoy together.

Dear Listener

I'm a divorced dad with custody of our two-year-old. When I take him to the park, I generally see the same kids and parents. We're all pleasant with each other if not overly friendly. One mother seems not to like me. I can't figure out why, but I decided not to worry about it. One day in the parking lot she told me I was using the car seat incorrectly. When I asked if she could show me how to do it correctly, she said she was too busy. Should I invite her for something to drink and talk to her?

Puzzled Dad

Dear Puzzled Dad

Only to tell her what a bitch she is. The fact that she would go out of her way to point out how you're endangering your child and then refusing to help you, indicates a level of bitterness no amount of chamomile tea will assuage.

Dear Listener

My brother lives in Austin, Texas, and is hosting a bat mitzvah for his only daughter. I live in California. As an overweight senior I have not traveled or attended indoor events since the pandemic. I would love to support my brother and niece, but I don't feel comfortable navigating airports, flying, or attending large indoor gatherings. My other brother told me if I don't go, I will "irreparably damage" my relationship with our other brother. What should I do?

Stuck Sibling

Dear Stuck

This is an example that blood is not thicker than water and is infinitely messier. Spring for a generous gift for your niece with a note to her and your brother about your concerns and regrets. Then send a note to your other brother that just says, "bite me."

Dear Listener

I am 22 and starting a new job in December. I just signed a lease on a tiny apartment. Previously, I've lived in dorms and student housing where people keep their doors open if they wanted to socialize. That doesn't seem right in an apartment building. So how do I make friends-

bake cookies and knock on doors? Maybe invite neighbors on a gallery walk? What do you think?

New Neighbor

Dear New Neighbor

I think you're asking to get murdered. Double lock your door and don't open it for anyone without a can of mace in your hand.

Dear Listener

My boyfriend comes from a wealthy family. Every year his parents take him and his siblings on an extravagant vacation. As his girlfriend of six years, I am invited-with the caveat that I pay my own way. But my boyfriend and I are graduate students so that's unrealistic. I can't even afford to split the costs with my boyfriend, which he's offered to do. These are long trips, booked in advance (like cruises and tours) so he can't leave early, and they use up most of his vacation time. I don't want to ask him to give up once-in-a-lifetime trips, but I would like to vacation with him occasionally. Any thoughts?

Stranded at home

Dear Stranded

Yes. During his next vacation, start looking for a new boyfriend. He's not going to marry you anyway. He's too tied to his family. They know you can't afford these vacations. If they really liked you and thought you'd be marrying their son they'd pay for you. I know you think you're getting married after grad school. Not gonna happen.

Dear Listener

I noticed that a former co-worker posted a creative project on his website. He is passing it off as his work without any other credit. The problem is, I came up with the idea and worked on it from start to finish. He was not involved at all. He pitched a vaguely related idea, but the company chose my pitch over his. And I brought it to life. Yet there it is,

sitting on his website. Should I speak up or let karma sort this out?

Miffed co-worker

Dear Miffed

Karma is so much more effective when accompanied by the threat of a

lawsuit.

Dear Listener

We just learned that our 13-year-old has to go back to school a week

early from band camp. I think he's responsible enough to stay in our

apartment alone for the week while the rest of the family stays at our

weekend home in the mountains. My husband disagrees. What do you

say?

Trusting Mom

Dear Trusting Mom

One question: Was it his idea to go to band camp or yours? If it was yours, DO NOT LEAVE HIM UNSUPERVISED. He will try to prove to his friends that he is not a dork for going to band camp, so he will invite a bunch of them to your house who will bring other friends and go nuts mixing Nyquil with lemonade unless they can get to your liquor cabinet. In any case, there will be vomit in your Wedgwood salad bowl when you return.

Dear Listener

I live in a larger cooperative apartment in New York City. During work hours I have seen a porter entering a neighbor's apartment in the morning several times over the past month. I believe they are "fooling around" while he is supposed to be working. Is it ethical to report this to the building superintendent or management?

Annoyed Neighbor

Dear Annoyed

Do you really have the time to monitor the comings and goings from your neighbor's apartment? How about getting a life? And just maybe her pipes are REALLY clogged.

Dear Listener

I have someone who has been a dear friend for 40 years. We live far apart and have kept in touch by text over the past fifteen years. A few years ago, we had a minor text argument and at some point, I suspected her husband of texting her, but I let it go. Recently we were planning a visit. The plans fell through and once again her texts seemed to be written by someone else. I asked her to call me, and she has not. I'm wondering if she is in some danger from her husband, who I suspect is continuing to return my texts, and I should be calling the police.

Concerned and Suspicious

Dear Concerned and Suspicious

Oh yeah, your friend is definitely dead. You needn't bother calling the police as her husband is probably in Mazatlan. He keeps texting to forestall you coming to visit—at least until the body completely decomposes.

Dear Listener

Our son and his fiancée, both 24, are getting married next summer. The bride's mother has commandeered the planning. When the kids express their opinion, she gets huffy and overrules them. Early on she asked my son, "Are your parents splitting the cost of the wedding with us?" Flustered, he said yes. But no one told us! Now the mother of the bride has planned an extravagant affair and sent us a spreadsheet with "our share" of the costs. We can't afford it. I think she is way off base. My wife wants us to take out a loan. Your thoughts?

Miffed Dad

Dear Miffed Dad

My first thought is that unless your son grows a pair, he's in for a miserable married life.

Dear Listener

I have a friend, 29, who chronically uses a "sexy baby" voice: high-pitched, syrupy, and incredibly jarring. She uses it for full sentences at a stretch. As women, we are often conditioned to speak like this, so I can see how she might use this voice when she feels uncomfortable or nervous. But this has been her default mode for years. I am embarrassed for her when I hear her talking to friends and strangers. Still, I may not be the best person to say something to her. I only see her a few times a month. How can I help her break this habit without offending her?

Helpful Friend

Dear Helpful

You can't. (I don't know what "sexy baby" is but "eeww"). After waiting all these years without saying anything she'll be either 1) defensive; 2) offended; or 3) embarrassed. Your call.

Dear Listener

I recently reconnected with a person from my past on whom I am now developing a major crush. The feeling is mutual which is great. But the other day we discovered that we share a much-loved therapist. I always wanted to date an evolved person who goes to a therapist-just not mine! I also get the sense that neither of us wants to find a new therapist. Help.

Not Fair to Share

Dear Not Fair

Next time either one of you has a session scheduled, go together. Tell the therapist that they have to decide which one to continue to treat. If they pick your crush, then run. They're crazier than you.

Dear Listener

I had a baby this spring and luckily, she gives me nothing to complain about. She sleeps well, hardly cries, and loves day care which has allowed me to go back to work. Several friends have babies the same ages as mine and they tell me how to struggle with sleep deprivation, separation anxiety and bad moods. How should I handle these talks without coming off as bragging about how easy my baby is so far.

Lucky Mom

Dear Lucky

1) Look up empathy in the dictionary.

2) Shut up about your kid.

Dear Listener

I am a 71-year-old widow with a caring new boyfriend of five months. We live in the same condo complex; it offers many (free) activities and clubs that we participate in. But when I suggest dates outside the condo he asks how much they will cost and suggest we go Dutch treat. I am confused by this. He receives a good pension and Social Security payments. I am willing to share costs but I would like to be the one who makes that decision. Your thoughts?

Old School Girlfriend

Dear Old School Girlfriend

Your school closed down a long time ago. Where do I begin? Are you privy to his complete financial situation? He may be very concerned about not outliving his money. Regardless of any of that, why is it your decision? Are you going to walk five steps behind him? Bind your feet? Looks like you'll be all set when 1953 comes around again.

Dear Listener

My sister travels frequently for work and always asks me to take care of her dog. I like the dog, but I work long hours and often go out in the evening. I don't want to take care of it every time she's away. I suggested she board the dog and even researched local kennels, but she refuses to do that. How can I say no without upsetting her?

Brother

Dear Brother

You can't. She's gotten a free ride for a while so there's no incentive for her to do anything different. The fact that you suggested, and even researched kennels tells her in no uncertain terms that you're looking to get out of this responsibility, but she clearly doesn't care. Speak up or you've got a lifetime of this, and just wait till she has kids.

Dear Listener

I moved to Los Angeles last year to sublet an apartment from a friend. A year later I'm still in the apartment and he's in that same far away city with a new wife, child, and enough work to ensure he will probably not come back. He told me to make the apartment my own. I mentioned selling some of the furniture and he didn't seem to care about the proceeds. The only thing he wants is a shelf of his records and books. So, can I sell his complete set of Breaking Bad DVDs on ebay?

Long Distance Friend

Dear Long-Distance Friend

"He didn't seem to care about the proceeds?" Did you say, "I'm going to sell everything except what you specifically said you wanted, and keep all the money for myself?" I'm guessing, no. I'm also guessing that you're asking me because you don't think you'll get the answer you want from him.

Dear Listener

Our outdoor hot tub will be delivered soon. My husband and I intend to use it during daylight and without wearing swimsuits. We have neighbors who live forty feet away and will be able to see us, if they choose to, when we walk the twenty-nine feet from our patio to the hot tub. We have some non-neighbor friends who are appalled by this. You?

Free Spirit

Dear Free

I doubt that I could care less. Why your friends would, I have no earthly idea.

Dear Listener

My husband and I own a vacation condominium (with two bedrooms and two bathrooms) that we like to make available to our five adult children. We don't use it over the holidays, but the kids' use of it during this period has become contentious. Four are married, one is divorced, and they all have children. It used to work out when three of the families wanted to spend a few nights there, but now all five of them want to use the condo over the 10-day Christmas break. We suggested shared usage or a rotation system, but this has resulted in sibling quarrels that are reported back to us for resolution. I know it's early for holiday questions, but can you help?

Mom

Dear Mom

You did say "adult" children? Okay, here's what you do: Let them each write you a letter telling you how wonderful you are, and how devoted they are to you. The best letter wins the condo stay and the other two are banished for life. (Yes, I've seen too many productions of King Lear). No good? Okay, let THEM figure it out-either everybody agrees, or nobody stays there.

Dear Listener

It is common now and seems to be acceptable to discuss other people's money. "He inherited a fortune," "I heard she's earning six figures." I don't want to participate in these conversations even if they are acceptable. How can I politely communicate this fact?

Hanging on to Decorum

Dear Hanging

I'd suggest excusing yourself by saying, "Sorry I have to go. I'm selling my blood at 3:30" and leave.

Dear Listener

My sister has fallen out with her daughter. Bad enough, but my niece is getting married soon, and my sister has asked all her siblings and their children not to attend the wedding. I don't know what to do. I really feel caught in the middle.

Anxious Aunt

Dear Anxious

What is this, junior high school? Of course, you feel caught in the middle. You, and whoever else your sister can get to, is using her appeal to loyalty as ammunition. You don't say what the falling out is over, but unless your niece left a burning cross on your sister's lawn, I'm betting they make up, and if you don't show, you're the bad aunt who didn't come to the wedding.

Dear Listener

My wife thinks (correctly) that I give her too much "helpful" advice-how to load the dishwasher, for instance, or avoid grammatical errors. I am trying to stop but lately she has taken to playing games on her phone when we socialize with other couples. She turns her body to hide what she's doing, but this seems so rude! I have held back from saying anything, given our issue, but may I say something this once?

Harried Husband

Dear Harried

One thing has nothing to do…never mind. If neither of you see the difference between your anal-retentive nagging and her willingly ignoring basic civility, there is no hope for your marriage. (Or you're perfect together)

Dear Listener

I live in a so-so rental building. Some of the neighbors on my floor have ratty doormats. So, I went out and bought new matching doormats for everyone—at my own expense. After I put them down, one of my neighbors threw the new mat away and put her old one back! How should I handle this?

Helpful Neighbor

Dear Helpful

I can't think of a better way to introduce yourself to people you don't know than trying to get rid of their possessions without asking them while insulting their taste and judgment. While you're at it, why not give them some advice on how to raise their children?

Dear Listener

My wife and I invited a new neighbor for dinner. She is accomplished, worldly and affluent. When she arrived, we were surprised that she brought nothing with her-no bottle of wine or flowers. It seemed to us she had broken the unspoken rule of bringing a host gift to a dinner party. We enjoyed ourselves, and she promised to reciprocate. When she does, my wife and I disagree about whether to bring a host gift. Your view?

Host

Dear Host

So let me get this straight: You think your dinner guest was impolite for not bringing anything with her to a dinner to which you invited her.

Your response is to accept her invitation and be (by your standards) impolite. Got it.

Dear Listener

My mother has a jar of pot gummies that she uses as a sleep aid. She doesn't know that I know about them. I have been keeping an eye on the jar. She doesn't seem to use many of them. Can I take a few gummies to sell to friends to pay for Hannukah gifts for my family?

Giving Daughter

Dear Giving

How nice that you want to buy gifts for your family. There's a word for what you want to do-it's STEALING. Why not rob a liquor store like any self-respecting thief?

Dear Listener

I just started using dating apps and I'm finding that most of the men have full beards. I don't like kissing men with facial hair. Is it ok if I meet someone I like, to ask them to shave?

Likes It Smooth

Dear Smooth

Sure. As long as you'd be okay if he asks you to get a Brazilian wax.

Dear Listener

My husband was chatting with our new neighbor when the neighbor mentioned he could see me undressing at night through my bathroom window. My husband was speechless, and I continue my nightly ritual which does not include drawing the shades. Was our neighbor wrong to say something? Shouldn't he just not look?

Nothing to Hide

Dear Nothing

Where to begin: Let's start with the question about your neighbor: As the public service announcement goes-he saw something, he said something-with the rationale that he thought you might not want to be seen. But that doesn't seem to be an issue for you. You clearly want to be seen because you have no intention of not exposing yourself. Why not just sell tickets and be done with it?

Muting My Own Horn

I seem innately predisposed to making myself invisible.

My email box overflows with messages from friends and acquaintances telling me about their latest projects and urging me to support them by attending their new performance, staged reading, or directorial accomplishment. When I get these messages, I always feel a combination of repulsion (by the blatant self-promotion); guilt (if I don't go); and admiration for the ability to do something I can't bring myself to do: Tell the world when a play I've written is being produced, or that there's a play in which I'm performing.

The emails I get about other people's work are relentless. I often want to reach through the ether and ask, "do you just push the SEND button every two days until your show sells out?" Or how about this: "I'll buy a ticket if you stop sending me emails." Even if I relent and buy a ticket online, because the guilt has overwhelmed me, or I really do want to support a friend, or (surprise!) I actually want to see the play- I STILL get these emails asking me to buy a ticket. Even if I send back a message saying that I'll be there, I still get the same appeal to buy a ticket every time the email is sent out.

Why do I have a problem telling people about my work? After all, in my small universe of local theatre, my work is generally well-received, I usually feel good about it, and yet I still have this reticence when it comes to promoting it.

I like to think of myself as the strong silent type. A man who needs no positive reinforcement. This makes no sense. You'd think that with all my insecurities (including fear of heights, doctors, physical pain, and abandonment), I'd do whatever I could to elicit praise.

Maybe this reticence comes from my father, a poor man's Borscht Belt comic, who often said to me "there's a reason you have an inferiority complex, son-you're inferior" (rim shot). In any event, I am constitutionally unable to generate a message that says, "I'm in this," or I've written this, come and see it."

The thing is, I really do want people to see my work, and tell me how wonderful it is (or else lie convincingly), but I just can't bring myself to ask them.

Although I make only occasional visits to the strange country of Facebookland, I can't help but notice that the number of promotional emails I get pale in comparison to the running commentary of my Facebook "friends" who detail the progress of every step leading up to the event they're promoting. First, it's getting the gig, then announcing the cast. Then we have to hear all about how rehearsals are going ("the most talented cast I've ever worked with"). Then, finally, the avalanche of posts about how great this show is, and how imperative it is that everyone go and see it.

Although I can't imagine promoting myself like this, it's clear that this is what's expected. Even necessary. Everybody is selling something all the time, which is mortifying to me. I was always taught that it's bad form to boast about yourself. But the reality is that if you want your work to be seen by someone other than your family, you've got to put it out there.

But I can't.

Occasionally, when I'm with friends, someone will ask if I'm working on a new project. This gives me permission to (modestly) talk about a short play of mine that was produced, or someone else's in which I had a role. At that point, they always say the same thing: "You should tell us when you're in a play. We'd love to come." That's my cue to adopt an "aw shucks" pose and tell them that I'm just bad at self-promotion "And anyway," I say, "everyone's so busy," or "it's too far away."

Finally, during one of these spasms of false modesty (because I did, in fact, love the opportunity to spew out my forthcoming credits) my friend, Michael said, "So what if it's inconvenient? Don't make the choice for us. Let us choose whether to show up or not."

Of course. Just provide information. No pleading.

I don't know why I hadn't seen this before, but it suddenly made perfect sense to me. I could let people know what I'm doing, with the full expectation that no one will show up. I won't bludgeon everybody to death with constant updates, but at least I'm doing something to promote my work.

Now, when I have a play coming up, I simply tell everyone I know that the show is happening. No appeals.

Even better, I wait until the producers or someone in the cast sends out a Facebook message about the project and I just share it.

If I'm feeling particularly daring, I go to my email list, attach the flyer for the show, and type the message "This is what I've been up to." I then go through my contacts fighting the urge to skip people for whom I think, "it's too far for them," or "they won't like this play," "I didn't show up at their birthday party, "they're anti-Semites" (Wait, what are they doing on my email list?). Then I close my eyes and push SEND.

Now when I see any of these people, I have a different problem. I have to weather an onslaught of comments like:

"Sorry I couldn't come. I was out of town"

"We were planning to come, but Brittany had an ear infection"

"I've just been so busy with (fill in the blank) I just couldn't make it."

See. I told you so.

So You Want to Get a Cat

Not so fast

I get it. You're lonely, cooped up most of the time and you have no friends. A pet will make you feel better. Especially a pet you don't have to walk. But what do you know about cats? Not a damn thing.

I understand the impulse. Unlike dogs, cats will not slobber all over you, or demand your undivided attention. On rainy, or excruciatingly hot days, or if it snows, you'll be glad you don't have to walk a cat. And the lure of having a furry, warm-blooded friend for the company is certainly appealing. However, there are a few things you might want to keep in mind before you make a commitment to a furry friend.

Ok. Let's start with the premise that you don't think a cat is a child that you will dress up, throw birthday parties for, and take with you everywhere you go. And conversely that you don't think a cat is like a stuffed animal that you ignore unless you're making your bed (If you never make your bed, please stop reading this and get a stuffed animal instead).

Assuming you don't fall into any of the above categories, you want to get a cat with whom you'll feel most compatible. While this is not an exhaustive list, it does paint a picture of what you'll find in the feline community. Just think of the following as "cat tinder."

Abyssinians

Highly intelligent and inquisitive. They love to explore and then carry off things that occupy their interest. They are very demanding. They will wait up for you and then grill you about where you were, who you were with, and why you've come home so late. Give them an unsatisfactory answer and you won't be able to find your wallet the next morning.

American Shorthair

A smart, moderately active feline. American Shorthairs enjoy learning tricks and challenging their intelligence with interactive toys. If your ego is easily bruised don't challenge an American Shorthair to scrabble or chess. They will kick your ass. They'll get along fine with a cat-friendly dog, but their hunting instincts may take over when it comes to pet birds or other small animals. Give away your pet gerbil unless you want to find its mangled carcass on your bed tomorrow morning.

Maine Coon

These cats are gentle-natured and friendly, making them excellent companions. They are the quintessential "curious cat" and will go through your dresser draws and desk. They will definitely read your diary. They are often tenderly playful--making them kitten-like throughout their lives. But they are HUGE. You should start working out if you plan on picking one up on a regular basis. And If you anger a Maine Coon, you could get smothered in your sleep.

Manx

The Manx is a loving, calm, and playful cat. They will even carry on a conversation with you in a soft, warbling voice. They're not interested in idle gossip or sports but will respond well to discussions of current events and culture. As a people-oriented cat, they need lots of attention so do not leave them alone for hours at a time or you will find an unpleasant surprise in your Manolo Blahniks. They're angry about not having a tail, so don't mention it.

Russian Blue

The Russian Blue is gentle, quiet, and shy around strangers, but affectionate and loyal toward her people. They are fastidious about personal habits. They'll attack anyone who comes into your house without taking their shoes off. They're very much a creature of routine, so if you don't get up in time to feed them breakfast, you may find that they have deleted everything you have DVR'd. They are tolerant of children unless the little dears tease them, in which case they will make withering comments designed to erode their self-confidence.

Himalayan

The Himalayan is a sweet and mild-tempered feline. They are affectionate but selective about who they choose to care about. They may be reserved around guests, especially those with opposing political views. Those with whom they violently disagree can expect to have a hairball thrown up in their lap. Serene, quiet environments with few day-to-day changes are best for the Himalayan. If you enjoy loud music, best not to get a Himalayan unless you want your cherished Van Briggle pottery to wind up in a thousand pieces on the floor.

After reading this, you may find that cat ownership might be too challenging for you. I'm not here to judge you.

There is no shame in owning a goldfish.

Zoom and Me
(December 2021)

I didn't look for this relationship, and never wanted it, but almost without realizing it, we were suddenly involved. For the most part, Zoom and I are a thing. I can't say it's exclusive. There are occasionally dates with GoTo Meeting and Google Hangouts. Initially, I thought this would be a casual, once in a while thing with Zoom. You know, a novelty, something different occasionally. Even when we started spending more time together last March, I thought it would be a temporary thing. Certainly, I never pictured a Zoom icon on my desktop. But here we are, almost two years later and we're spending almost all our time together.

From what I can determine Zoom seems pretty happy with the arrangement. They (Zoom's preferred pronoun) occasionally have their moments as we all do, and I'm subjected to a silent treatment or a complete disconnect from me. But I can weather these occasional lapses. The truth is, that with this pandemic we're together ALL THE TIME and frankly, it's exhausting. While they were okay in small doses, the effect of seeing small faces in small boxes and hearing voices only filtered through the internet has ceased to be amusing. And there's no letup. They're with me at work, when I'm with family and friends.

I thought I would be able to get some distance by escaping into my creative pursuits. But Zoom is there as well, mocking me by providing a clear transmission of my colleague's work while waiting until my work is being read and then disconnecting. Only leaving a silent, blank screen, so I can contemplate the hold they have on me.

As I zoomed on to Zoom play readings by local theatres, the deficiencies I hadn't noticed when they were "live "seemed to increase, or maybe they hadn't, and I was just "Zoomed Out."

Lest you think I'm breaking up with Zoom let me disabuse you of that notion. Sheltering in place and being a member of the high-risk group has severely curtailed my options in connecting with other humans.

I started to contemplate re-evaluating my relationship with Zoom. It wasn't Zoom's fault. Zoom had been loyal and reliable. I didn't want to leave Zoom for another platform, just another medium, like, maybe a podcast once in a while. As I was about to engage Zoom with the "it's not you, it's me" approach, I had a realization. Zoom is the only thing that gives me a connection, however tenuous, to other people. And even though I only see a part of them and hear a facsimile of their voice, it's something. It's something that reminds me there are still people out there who want to engage and keep connected to me and other humans.

I don't know what the future holds for my relationship with Zoom (we've tacitly agreed not to discuss it), but I've resolved to practice some self-care, including some alone time.

In the meantime, we'll continue to see each other, with the understanding that in the fullness of time things may change. If and when that time comes, we'll deal with it then.

Food Fighting...With Myself

I've come to an age where I have to pay attention to what I eat. How do I know this? Because of the various "ists" in my life. I collect medical specialists like I collected baseball cards in my youth. Currently, I'm under the care of a cardiologist, a nephrologist, a urologist, an internist, a neurologist, a podiatrist, an orthopedist, a gastroenterologist, and, of course, a psychiatrist. I also see a chiropractor who doesn't get an "ist" because he didn't go to medical school- although he's just as good.

What they've all said is that I have to watch what I eat. Which doesn't mean that I'm to take pictures of each meal and post them on Facebook. Rather, if I want to stay healthy as I enter my later years, I need to maintain a healthy diet.

Long gone are the days of my youth when the only thing that mattered when it came to food was how it tasted, how much I liked it, and how much of it I could I eat before I'd explode.

It's like the old joke: "I'm on a seafood diet. I see food. I eat it."

But my new healthy way of eating has changed everything. As a consequence, I'm always hungry for food I'm not allowed to eat.

As soon as I see someone eating on screen, I completely lose the thread of the story and focus on the risotto or the pie ala mode they're enjoying. Most people fast forward through commercials because they want to get back to the program. I do it so that I don't see commercials for Dairy Queen, which makes me want to reach through the television and grab one of those Blizzards.

I can't look at a restaurant menu without calculating the potential damage to my arteries and cholesterol level. Every order comes after a Hamlet-like internal struggle between what I want and what I know I should be eating. Last week I stopped at a diner to grab a quick bite. By now, I know what I can eat in a diner that will be relatively healthy and at least somewhat enjoyable. But, on this occasion, there was a young man sitting in a booth across from mine who I could clearly hear ordering a cheeseburger, fries, and a milkshake. I was able to put his order out of my head until his food arrived. As I picked at my egg white and spinach omelet, I could not take my eyes off the juicy meat, golden-brown potatoes, and frosty shake that he was eating. In a fit of Schadenfreude, I tried to make myself feel better by imagining him becoming obese after accumulating a series of debilitating health issues.

It didn't work.

The internet is no escape. I find myself clicking on sites I know I should not be looking at. Given the care that my wife takes to prepare meals that are good for me, she would probably be hurt if she knew I was ogling pictures of seven-layer cake, chili dogs, and pizza. I know I shouldn't look but sometimes I can't help myself.. The images alone cause me to salivate like Pavlov's pooch. I have tried to stay away, but when I land on a site that shows a fluffy Mac and Cheese, in my not-so-healthy heart, I want it.

I should admit that I have slipped from time to time. At a friend's barbecue, my wife saw me looking lovingly at the grill filled with plump hot dogs and sausages. Unable to resist, I scooped one up and before I was done, grabbed a second one.

I know my wife didn't approve but she and I have an understanding - as long as I don't make a habit out of it, or do it at home, she accepts my occasional straying from healthy eating.

I've really tried to stop, but unfortunately, the longings persist.

Maybe I should just stay off the internet.

Or I could just watch porn.

About the Author:

Bronx-born and bred, Ed is commitment-phobic when it comes to literary forms as he flits from short plays to short non-fiction, and to short fiction (at least he's got the short thing down). He took up playwrighting during an interminable time spent backstage while playing the Pedant in a community theatre production of Taming of the Shrew. Ed's plays have had forty staged productions throughout the NY metropolitan area, and around the country. His anthology Short Plays for Long Lives is published by Blue Moon Press. Ed's monologues are included in the anthologies, Mother/Daughter Monologues: Midlife Catharsis (Gloria) and Urgent Maturity (Sarah) published by the International Centre for Women Playwrights. His monologue, Hannah, is published in Best Women's Monologues for 2019. His play The Keys to Life has been adapted for the screen into a film of the same title by the Northern Virginia Film Co-op and is shown at independent film festivals.

His prose has been seen in The New Croton Review, Slackjaw, Flash Fiction Magazine, Mocking Owl Roost, Bright Flash Literary Review, Fleas on the Dog, The Haven, Crow's Feet, Best of Potato Soup Journal, Submittable, Door is a Jar, Bronx Memoir Project, Shady

Grove Literary, Fresh Words, Libretto Magazine, Wicked Shadow Press, and The Bad Day Book.

Ed spent over 30 years in parallel careers serving the arts community, and older adults and their families. He has directed programs at senior centers and home care providers, and created and led a caregivers' support group in the Bronx. As Deputy Director at the Bronx Council on the Arts, Ed played a leadership role in the formulation of policy and programming, advocacy, grantmaking, and community development. He later became the co-founder and first Executive Director of Lifetime Arts, a non-profit organization that encourages creative aging by promoting the inclusion of arts education programs in organizations that serve older adults.

He received a B.A. in Psychology from Hunter College and an M.A. in Liberal Studies from Empire State University.

Ed resides in Peekskill, New York which is the furthest he's ever lived from Yankee Stadium.

Made in the USA
Middletown, DE
03 September 2024

59613396R00132